Connecticut Beautiful

Connecticut Beautiful

BY

WALLACE NUTTING

Author of States Beautiful Series, etc.

ILLUSTRATED BY THE AUTHOR WITH THREE
HUNDRED AND FOUR PICTURES COVERING
ALL THE COUNTIES IN CONNECTICUT

Bonanza Books • New York

FOREWORD

WHEN the author began to plan for this book, he looked about to learn whether there was anything of the sort ever issued, and found that many parts of the state of Connecticut had been illustrated and described; but that there was no general work which gave many pictorial representations. The state is certainly worthy of a fuller recognition in this particular. There are enthusiasts who claim that Connecticut is more beautiful than New Hampshire.

Although the author has lived eight years in Connecticut and has a strong partiality for it, he feels it may be safer to take the ground that Connecticut has peculiar beauties all her own, different from those of other states. We could not get on without Connecticut nor do we wish to try. She has no such extremes of contour as the more mountainous states of New England but her peculiar geologic formations, her extensive bound on Long Island Sound, her reach of highlands on the Connecticut, are of sufficient distinction to win attention and regard. But to our thought, it is the country homes of Connecticut that constitute her greatest charm.

The author has obtained some assistance in little poems on country lanes which have been specially made for the particular pictures opposite which they stand, and with which the name of the author appears.

There are those in northern New England who are of the general impression that Connecticut fills in the space between Massachusetts and New York and that, as they pass over it on the night train, it is probably solid ground; but, as to seeing anything of it, the idea will be new to many. We are ready to maintain, however, that given a month of vacation time, it may be spent as happily and instructively in Connecticut as in any other like area of America. Further, we are ready to declare that

3

there are various aspects of American life to be found in Connecticut and nowhere else. We can never cease to be thankful for the conservatism of Connecticut. Without that well-reasoned conservatism, we should have lost very much of the highest importance. Connecticut is a museum of late seventeenth and early eighteenth century American life. Her numerous historical societies have done far more than Massachusetts or, indeed, any other state in keeping for us the examples and the records of what is very old.

Connecticut being a state of moderate dimensions and somewhat dense population, it is feasible for those whose scintillating intellects demand city arenas in which to disport themselves to live in the country and work in town.

We here anticipate a regret that will be expressed from many quarters at not discovering in this volume pictorial records of all parts of the state. Limitations of space have prevented the use of various pictures which may possibly stimulate the production of a second volume on this state. We can only say that we have included all that we could. We have also made use of a considerable number of old house sketches which are drawn from our original photographs.

If the reader understands our intention, he will be inclined to bid us God-speed. We make no pretentions to exhaustive treatment of any part of the state or to superior knowledge. We only seek to bring before you much that no one person would have found without rather extensive observation.

WALLACE NUTTING

Framingham, Massachusetts

To

THE CONNECTICUT HISTORICAL SOCIETY
TO WHOSE COLLECTIONS AND ARCHIVES
OF SUCH GREAT VALUE THIS LITTLE
COLLECTION OF CONNECTICUT PICTURES OF
SMALL ACCOUNT IS GRATEFULLY ADDED

Connecticut Beautiful

• •

CONNECTICUT

CONNECTICUT stands alone in having preserved for America many of the finest traditions, not only in politics and religion, but in mechanical excellence wedded to good taste. She kept for at least fifty years longer than other parts of the country the quainter and more characteristic forms of construction in the domestic arts and architecture. Connecticut landscapes are more definitely defined as early American scenes than any other part of our land, because in the country districts where old houses abound, the hewn overhang of hundreds of her dwellings still remains. The settlers of Connecticut were marked from the first as abounding in mechanical ability. Having also with this ability a love for the fine old lines of construction which their fathers had followed, they have kept for our admiration and our financial impoverishment many wonderful old examples. Of the framed overhang houses, four out of the twelve known in America are in one village of Connecticut, — Farmington. Of the stately court cupboards which have come down to us, probably at least two-thirds have been found in Connecticut; and we can state from personal experience that their owners seem determined that they shall remain there.

The state, being the part of New England next to New York, has in these later days contributed largely to that part of New York where ingenuity is matched with capital. Particularly in metal work of the finer quality Connecticut has always been preeminent. Mostly those products of brass, which we ought to call bronze for romance' sake, are made in Connecticut; and those that are made elsewhere are mostly made by Connecticut men. The seamstress and the sportsman look to Connecticut to supply a great part of those ingenious or precise inventions which mark modern life.

The settlers of Connecticut, while quite similar in their points of view, nevertheless were politically separated into two parts centering respectively in Hartford and New Haven. There was a conservatism about their customs and even their laws which has been talked up and cried down under the name " blue laws."

Connecticut, particularly, gave its cast of mind to the Western Reserve, that portion of Ohio which is now much more populous and much richer than its source, containing as it does the great city of Cleveland with its million inhabitants and its vast and diversified manufacturing, largely in metals, the work in which was first inspired by the immigrant from Connecticut.

The contour of Connecticut presents delightfully pleasing features of sufficient divergence in type to interest the traveler. The Connecticut highlands from Middletown southeast, pierced by the river, are not surpassed perhaps by any similar stretch of river scenery in our country, or, if surpassed, they are so by the Hudson Highlands alone.

The geologic formation of western Connecticut affords many sharp and abrupt breaks in the hills which dominate and give character to the landscape, and add immeasurably to its beauty. It is hard to find anywhere more beautiful drives than those we see from Hartford through Waterbury and Danbury to Norwalk; from Hartford northwest through Winsted to the Berkshires; from Hartford easterly past Bolton Notch to Willimantic and thence to Norwich and New London. Then, of course, there is the famous shore drive from the bounds of New York City to Rhode Island which passes a multitude of quaint houses, charming inlets, and alternate glimpses of hill and sound.

A HEWN OVERHANG—MADISON

These are only a part of the more beautiful Connecticut routes. One may go on from Willimantic to Putnam and Worcester; or one may pass through Stafford Springs by the new route being opened in the hill towns to Southbridge. The main route north and south through the state: entering from Longmeadow in the north, passing through Hartford, and so on to New Haven is not in its lower reaches as winning as some other drives but the upper section, through the remarkably rich river lands, is an unusual experience in a New England drive.

Were we to sum up the most distinctive and most attractive features of Connecticut, we should say that for quaintness the state is unsurpassed; for scenic beauty it ranks very high; for specialized mechanical genius of its people it is unequalled. The old Connecticut resident is well satisfied with his surroundings and with his own capacity to make use of them. He has an alert witty mind, is well read, and, from the vantage ground of his ancient state and fine traditions, reaches out to know and to appraise critically the rest of the world.

SOUTHWESTERN CONNECTICUT

GREENWICH is the first town in the state as one comes from New York, and it has taken on, perhaps, too much the character of citified estates. It vies with Westchester County in New York in the extent and elaborateness of its dwellings, some of them rejuvenated farm houses, but most of them frankly new dwellings. The habit of copying the southern type of dwellings, which have their chimneys on the outside, has come into Connecticut of late more than it was found in the earlier days. As one goes north, one meets more and more the sort of roof found in Holland. That is to say, the gambrel type does not serve well where heavy snows fall, as the upper portion of the gambrel is too flat, and, in the case of a thaw, the water backs up under the shingles and soon causes a leaky roof. The chimneys, also, are needed in the interior of the dwellings in the latitude of New England, and the ancient instances of external chimneys are extremely rare.

That in the old stone house at Guilford, which is publicly owned, and is looked upon as a seventeenth century example of the highest importance, shows its chimney on the outside. This probably arose from the circumstance that the builder came from a warmer district. Other cases of the Dutch type are found here and there along the coast: the most northern one we have observed being near New Haven.

Greenwich is very beautiful by nature, and is becoming more and more finished by the hand of man. Its higher lands offer a somewhat wide prospect. The spire of the Congregational church is a landmark on Long Island Sound. Near by is the series of broken natural steps, down which Putnam dashed when he escaped from the British.

PINK, BLUE, AND GREEN—NORWALK

FROM THE HILL—FAIRFIELD

ENTICING WATERS—BROAD BROOK

A HOMESTEAD ON THE NAUGATUCK

The road onward to Norwalk is dotted with old houses, and all the side roads are interesting. As we go a little north from Norwalk, we come upon a pool (p. 11) with wild apple trees about one bank, and fine elms and maples on the opposite side. This picture and others made near the same spot are among the author's most loved subjects. The slightly wrinkled surface of the water, in this instance, conveys that much-to-be-desired quality of beauty which water surfaces often lack.

A DURHAM OVERHANG

That is to say, an unruffled placidity forms a mirror which is in no wise artistic, as one merely gets a double. It is necessary to wait for the slight kiss of a gentle wind. Sometimes we have found it useful to disturb the waters at the edge and allow gentle ripples to undulate across the pool, which is otherwise too still. But if the wind rises to disturb the surface thoroughly the effect is in no respect artistic. There are no broken reflections or long lights, in such a case, as here have been retained.

This little valley and the parallel road slightly east of it, which runs to Wilton, have each many little streams and pools and orchards, which feed our love for the cosy and quiet retreats so suitable for country homes.

Norwalk itself is a beautiful village. South Norwalk being the business district, it is necessary to leave the main street a little to find the charms of the two Norwalks.

THE FALLS AT PUTNAM

A FAIRFIELD LANE

IN TENDER LEAF—CHESHIRE

NEARING HOME—NEWTOWN

The drive to New Canaan from South Norwalk, returning to Stamford or to Darien, reveals a series of roadsides consisting of hills of fair outline along the bases of which, on Five Mile River and in New Canaan, are numerous good early houses which have been so long at home here that they seem almost to blend with the soil from which they spring.

It is an intimate valley that we follow, going from Norwalk up the Norwalk River through Wilton to Danbury. The stream is in many places almost ideal in its broadening silent coves and winning curves. Whether at apple blossom time, when it is perhaps at its best; or in June at its next best, or in Autumn, this little journey is one which should not be forgotten.

All this section of Connecticut is very old. In fact, Connecticut affords us what we cannot find elsewhere, in an abundance of simple farmsteads of the earliest type, together with attractive backgrounds.

The old post office at Durham (see page 14), we have not been able to date. The corner, however, with a side and end overhang, as shown above, is very remarkable as a continuation of the earliest American style.

The entire establishment, consisting of this wing and the dwelling beyond, which, while old, is apparently somewhat later, is one of enticing interest. We do not know whether this overhang originally had beam projections finished as drops. However, it goes in general character with the dwellings in Farmington, which are the only ones known in Connecticut in this style; and the only ones in America, with the exception of eight in eastern Massachusetts.

As one journeys from Norwalk easterly, the Saugatuck River with its village; and northerly, on the same stream, the village of Westport call us to pause. Running up the river from Westport on the western bank for a few miles, and returning by the eastern bank, several attractive vistas appear.

Enticing Waters (page 12) shows fine tree arches. Broad Brook abounds in such scenes.

The town of Fairfield, next east of Westport, includes as much that is beautiful as any town in the state. Starting north from the village up Mill River, and swinging left to Greenfield Hill, one reaches there as wonderful a region for its fine highland farm land, close to the shore, as we know anywhere. It is in this drive that one passes the marvelous rows of flowering dogwood in alternating pink and white. The view of these trees is worth a very long journey. While they are not, perhaps, superior to apple blossoms, the white trees, at their climax, are the most dazzling assemblage of pure color that our climate produces. Greenfield Hill itself must in time come to be recognized for what it is, a fascinating beautiful residence district. The roads beyond, toward Aspetuck, are in summer safe and are quaintly studded with early dwellings. Returning by the way of Cricker Brook and thence down to Mill River, we find there a valley of fine orchards, and water stretches.

On page 15, we show a Fairfield lane. There was a soft haze and the atmosphere was moist. It was impossible to see very far, but there were ghostly blossoming trees in the middle distance, and beyond all was a mystery. Of course this lane led to an enchanted valley, but the

SUMMER WIND — SOUTHBURY

AN OLD FASHIONED VILLAGE—LITCHFIELD COUNTY

A CHIMNEY AT EACH CORNER—TALCOTTVILLE

A STRATFORD HEWN OVERHANG

enchantment was in believing more than in exploring. How fortunate it is that we always remain children, and can always find in the lane beyond the hill, where no dwelling is visible, a city of the soul, bowered with delight, fair with all blooms, and endless charm of roof outlines, and fantastic foliage on the hillside. We did dare wander on a little, and came upon the old cellar of a small dwelling now vanished. The early blossoms hovered close about, cherry trees stood in the angles of the walls, and there were traces of a path which led down to the brook.

One may require some days, and may enjoy some weeks, in treading all the appealing roads about Fairfield and Westport. It will be observed that all western Connecticut lies in ridges running north and south, with sharp declensions, and always brooks between. One cannot go five miles from the shore without reaching a neighborhood as completely old in every aspect, saving some minor repairs on dwellings, as could have been seen two hundred years ago. It is not until we get away from the

[Continued on page 25]

THE ORCHARD LANE

Written for the picture opposite by MILDRED HOBBS

Bird-haunted, song enchanted,
Blossom-covered trees,
Fairies must have floated past you
On a friendly breeze.

Petal showers from bird-bowers
Softly drift and fall,
Tangled with the weed and brier
Of a tumbled wall.

Stems slender, bluettes tender,
Dainty shapes of Stars,
Peeping through the rustic ruins,
Kiss the broken bars.

Bloom-laden, like a maiden
Spreading out her gown,
Boughs of blossom sweep the borders
Of the road to town.

But there to beauty winding,
Lures on a narrow lane,
Flecked with golden dandelions,
Grassy ridges twain!

Friend yonder, come and wander!
Roads are blossom-spanned!
Let an orchard lane entice you
Into Fairyland!

HOME LANE — WOODBURY

LINGERING WATERS—CHESHIRE

A MAPLE IN MAY—LITCHFIELD COUNTY

AN OLD STRATFORD GABLE

centers beyond, we will say, the third mile of distance, that we begin to find things as they were, and perhaps ever shall be.

Fairfield itself, in its central portion, still preserves several excellent early dwellings, and the same is true of the contiguous village of Southport. We are almost ready to say that any brook in southern Connecticut is worth following up, if a road skirts it. The quick rise of the hills, hereabout, adds very much to the landscape, which thus has three charms: the nearby Sound, the meandering streams, and the sharply lifting verdured slopes.

In Tender Leaf (page 16) is one of the most winning water scenes the writer has found. It is at a little fork in the road where a right hand turn runs to Southington Mountain. It is now impossible to obtain any picture at this point owing to advertising signs which have defaced a wonderful beauty spot. We presume it is better policy, and in fact a necessity of private ownership, that advertisements should be allowed on private land. The only thing we can do, is to endeavor to tone up public sentiment till people shall be so far proud of their neighborhood as to do nothing against its attractiveness.

One may find a winding side road running down the Housatonic River. This old road is now lost to us with the flooding of a great area for power purposes. There were charming river sides with huge old buttonwood trees. We understand that these trees are no longer found to any extent in young growths. They are among the most beautiful, in branches and foliage. Their large leaves are very decorative and the bark, being in three colors, reminds one of the madrona in California. It is as if there were three garments on these exquisite boles. If the buttonwood tree is to die out of New England we must go south to find it.

In Summer Wind (page 19), we have an example of what can be done on an old estate in the way of redeeming its worst features and making them attractions. Where this pool now exists, there was a swampy bit of brook with unsightly bushes. The owner, in order to see across to the distant road, from time to time lopped off the tops of the bushes; and the space was possessed by one of the most unsightly swamps imaginable. The house became a byword for shabbiness and dismal surroundings. The erection of a dam just below the dwelling created this dear little pool in which, as one approached, the homestead was reflected with its fine trees, and became much admired. It was here that the author first began his work in picturing old-fashioned interiors, apple blossoms, streams and autumnal glories.

Another advantage of creating this small body of water was, that in making the dam wide enough for a drive, an outlet was secured to the main road, which permitted the giving up of the road nearer the dwelling except as a private approach. Thus, in effect, the fine knoll and its buildings were thrown back several hundred feet from the highway and became, not only more beautiful but more secluded.

Following the humorous story of the person whose andirons cost a fortune, because they stimulated other improvements, the author, having secured this central object of beauty for his homestead, proceeded to create another pool of about the same dimensions, on the left of the

UNDER THE BLOSSOMS—SOUTHBURY

DRAPED IN BLOSSOMS—OLD MYSTIC

THE MAPLE SUGAR CUPBOARD

THE LAST FURROW—NEWTOWN

PUBLIC EDIFICE—COLCHESTER

dwelling and on the other side of the road. Thus, from whatever quarter
the home place was approached, it could never be otherwise than beautiful. In a case like this, where water can be brought to approach near the
foot of a tree, the charm is greatly enhanced by the irregular contour, as
well as by the added charm of broken reflections. We were very careful
not to destroy the old walls of field stone, but only to repair them so far
as to make them able to stand securely. Stones of the same character,
only of greater dimensions, were used at the entrance, and the wall was
continued on the winding approach to the right.

Not only was this pool attractive as seen, but one could not go ten
feet around its margin, in any direction, without securing new outlines
and different reflections. That this statement is not the author's fancy
was proved, because the public showed itself in hearty accord. The opposite view shows the bridge and its flanking elms. The right angle
view shows the dwelling with its pines and locusts.

We take to ourselves no special credit for perspicacity, because there
are thousands of country places that could be improved in the same, or
in equally good ways. We only wonder why it isn't done.

The dwelling on page 21 has, we believe, been now renovated. It has that much to be desired chimney with a T or an L, that is, an extra flue added at the rear, which gives it a quaint effect. There is also the hewn over-hang on the second story, and on the gable an arrangement which tended to keep a dwelling warm, by preventing a drizzle of rain from falling down the whole length of the wall, and also to preserve it from decay. The lean-to is an obvious addition. The interior is beautifully panelled.

The Old Fashioned Village (page 20) is one of those examples where half a dozen houses congregate for company, and the cross roads curve into one another.

At Talcottville is a brick house with a chimney at each corner, as shown on page 20. This arrangement is also seen in a fine house at Norwich. It is very appealing from the sense of solidity imparted, and also for economy of construction: because, obviously, there are eight corner fire-places within, secured without breaking a wall, and with only one line to mark their interior faces. A corner fireplace is always attractive.

The old gable on page 25 has a curiosity in the form of a hinged window at the peak. That is to say, there is a casement. The house is otherwise interesting for its stone chimney, and for its second lean-to added to the first.

On page 24 we have an instance of red foliage in the spring, under the title A Maple in May. The spring coloring, where maples grow, is al-most as gorgeous as that of the Autumn, though this remark applies more particularly to the water maple otherwise called the soft or swamp maple.

Lingering Waters (page 24) has a strong appeal in its tree, draped with vines. This appeal is not less strong because of the dense shadows that lay along the trunk.

A portion of Connecticut, beginning at Greenwich and following the shore to the mouth of the Connecticut, shows not a little Dutch in-fluence. The Dutch of Manhattan established themselves here and there in this district, and erected quaint little dwellings which have always

BROOKSIDE BLOOMS—MANCHESTER

DELL DALE ROAD — WINDHAM COUNTY

HOMESTEAD BLOSSOMS — MYSTIC

DOORWAY AT HAMPTON

appealed to Americans as being the most interesting order of early architecture on a small scale. We do not remember to have seen such dwellings in Holland but the Dutch, like the English, adapted their architecture
to the new world, and, in the case of the little cottage with the roof
swept out in a curve over the porch, the effect was very winning. New
England is thus enriched in this corner at least by a marked variant of
its usual Colonial type, so much so that it has practically all the variations
of American architecture. In this respect Connecticut is richer than any
other state.

Under the Blossoms (page 27) calls to every aspect of our thought.
The farmer may see here the economic side of life; the lover of animals
is attracted by the sheep and lambs; the spring blossoms remind us of the
bridal season, and their promise of a harvest affords the comfortable
sense of plenty. The author kept these sheep for aesthetic reasons
purely, coaxing them about over the fields, here and there, to pose for their

portraits. This was the only manner in which they could be induced to pay their way, as their wool hardly paid for clipping. The same was true of the apple tree for the fruit of which we were offered, by the bushel, the same price asked for a single apple at a fruit stall in New York City. Thus we solved the problem — *Does Farming Pay?*

To those who are desirous of photographing sheep a hint may be acceptable. The scene should be selected beforehand and the bounds outlined. A little feed such as sheep especially love should be scattered on the grass, at the point where it is desired to induce them to stop. Then, all being ready, the sheep are headed in the direction required. This is very important; for in feeding away from the picture, they never pause a moment. In approaching, however, they hesitate from timidity to come nearer than is desired. The time required for picturing sheep is about a thirty-fifth of a second on a bright day. It is not feasible, therefore, to obtain sheep pictures on dull days. We have an otherwise perfectly good picture of sheep with five legs, although the time was a twenty-fifth of a second.

We have often been troubled by animals that were too tame. Calves, particularly, investigate artists' boxes for meal and salt. A curious situation arose in a certain district where painters in oil were forbidden to paint in the fields. A careless artist left behind him a paint-saturated rag which was tasted by an inquisitive cow with the consequence that she departed this life under painful circumstances. This was in the neighborhood of Mystic. As a rule, however, farmers are very much interested in picture people, and sometimes gather around with their families in embarrassing numbers. As a rule they often desire to be included in the picture and, as it is almost impossible for them to keep their eyes from the camera, the results are not satisfactory. When they go about their work in the fields their unconscious posing is good.

Draped in Blossoms (page 27), a sketch on a thoroughly back woods road, gave us a couple of interesting hours. The lone woman of the dwelling was delighted to see us working about and selecting the attrac-

A LITCHFIELD PORCH

LOCUST COTTAGE—MYSTIC

DELL BLOSSOMS—NEWTOWN

SUMMER GROTTO—BROAD BROOK

tive viewpoints, which had long been loved by her alone. The sharing of pleasures certainly doubles them. In fact, many pleasures entirely stale upon us unless we can show them to others. It requires a pair of congenial souls to enjoy obtaining pictures. Thus the getting them and the having them are both delightful.

The Maple Sugar Cupboard (page 28), made in our old Connecticut home in Southbury, represents a home room, as we call it, toward which our hearts hark back. It was just large enough and high enough for comfort. A great stone formed the hearth, and the walls of the fireplace itself were constructed of hewn granite. In the form of gneiss, it splits readily, requires little hammering and is full of glistening particles of mica. The height here under the beams is about seven feet. A room like this, about fourteen by twenty-six, with book shelves at one end, a turf door on the side, a porch of glass, and windows on two other sides that catch the sun all day, is as good a winter retreat as Florida. This is the room which first became well known as the scene of the author's so-called Colonial pictures. It is a good instance to illustrate the broad effects obtained by a low ceiling. Let the ceiling be carried up two feet higher and the room would lose all its charm, beside being much more difficult to heat. We placed in the chimney flue here a home made damper so that, if the fire on the hearth was ever permitted to die down, a draft could be avoided. In such a room any sort of a rug is appropriate so that its colors are agreeable. One may mix the braided and the hooked rugs, or the hooked rugs and Turkish rugs, but braided rugs form too strong a contrast with Oriental rugs. Large rugs are more desirable by far. The effect of many patches is bad.

Plowing among blossoms is a poetic occupation as The Last Furrow, on page 28. The region between Bridgeport and Newtown is most delightful in the blossom season and, even later on, it shows many fine rows of clumps of elms.

Newtown is not a sophisticated village, but owing to its elevation, it may yet be sought. Located as it is at a junction of three roads: those

to Bridgeport, Danbury and Waterbury, it is a convenient touring headquarters. The recent lake created by the dam at Zoar on the Housatonic has added immensely to the beauty of this region. When the river
was low in the old days it lost most of its charm. We know no finer sites
for dwellings than those to be found on the lofty hills on both sides of
the Housatonic. Following this stream up to New Milford, being prepared for ordinary roads, one will find at Pomperaug a river scene of
wonderful attractions. Not far below New Milford there are cliffs and
falls and evergreen groves. This is a neighborhood as yet unspoiled. In
these north and south valleys of Connecticut we often find a neighborhood
which, somewhat removed from the railway, follows fashions in life
that were good hundreds of years ago and are good still.

We have long since learned that, instead of scorning backward neighborhoods, we ought to cherish them. The mill village which is precisely
like the next one is not intriguing, but every district which has escaped
manufacturing has individuality. One cannot resist speculating on the
joy of obtaining from some of these old acres, just as nine generations of
ancestors have done, all the necessities of life, and most of the joys that
are worth having. The newspapers told us recently of a young wife
married in New York City to an ex-service man whose home was in Ohio.
As they started on their journey she attempted on the ferry boat, so the
item stated, suicide by poison and drowning. The reason she gave was that
she could not bear the thought of leaving the White Way. Personally
we should be tempted to commit suicide if we were confined to that
White Way. So humanity takes its choice. There is only so much that
can be gotten into life. Certainly independence and beauty as God made
it, and health giving air cannot be had on the White Way.

Blossoms At The Bend on page 31 is an instance of what is always
beautiful, a stream winding about an orchard. It is almost as rare as
beautiful.

Over The Wall (page 31) is the approach by a lane with a turn to a
hill farm. What has Broadway that can rival this? When men choose

BLOSSOMS AT THE BEND—TALCOTTVILLE

OVER THE WALL—NEWTOWN

THE WOODBURY-SOUTHBURY ROAD

the worst as the best, and despise the best as the worst, it is time to turn society over, for the cities are too top heavy. What do the residents beyond the blossoms do in winter? They take a sleigh ride and the fashionable city folks come to enjoy it.

The village of Litchfield, which improved on its English namesake by adding a " T," being situated at the end of a railway branch among the hills called here after Litchfield, a continuation of the Berkshire hills, ranges itself with Norfolk, Sharon and Woodstock as among the finer upland sights of Connecticut.

There are a good many doors in the village as fine as the two on page 32. As this book, however, is not devoted to architecture, we merely glance at a few of the rare and numerous old Connecticut houses. The great Whipping Post Elm would be worth remembering for its dignity alone. A town made famous by the Beechers and the site of a famous law school has, thus, great traditions as well as natural beauty and fine air. What more is required to make a town? Of course, all Litchfield residents recognize this and live up to it.

The period of many of the dwellings here was that of excellent taste though, for our part, we think that 1730 was even better than 1760. Within the doors of these old homes there is much good mahogany, and an occasional earlier piece; but the town was too thrifty, and had too much respect for itself, to preserve the quainter furniture before mahogany.

The width of the streets and the dignity of the dwellings form a unique combination. There are not lacking interesting old shops and byways that invite the investigator.

A Litchfield Porch (page 35) is a portion of the famous old Walcott mansion. The story goes that the old squire was sometimes called upon at unusual hours to perform marriage ceremonies. It is said that he would drop a window of the porch and perform the ceremony, while the couple waited lined up on the other side of the window. Anyway it was a good story.

That much to be desired butterfly table, which is supposed to have had its first ancestor in Connecticut, appears with other good things upon the porch; but the fine colonial lines of the arch, together with its vines, supply us with a choice bit of the old days.

The Walcott family is famous in the annals of Connecticut and of the whole nation. It is much to say of a town that the fine old family homestead of the Walcotts is only one among many.

The dweller in Locust Cottage (page 35), near Mystic, loved his old home so much that he is said to have left it but seldom. The picture is an execellent instance of the charm that may be secured by sheer simplicity. The lines of the house are absolutely plain. They could not be more so. Yet, flanked as they are by foliage, they have a powerful appeal that few attempt to resist. Let the prospective builder take notice how little he requires to secure charm. One may indeed say that age is

OVER THE LANE—LONG HILL

BOWERED — WATERBURY

A LITTLE OLD HOME — NORWALK

HOUSE ON NEW BRITAIN-HARTFORD ROAD

necessary to give mellowness. Happily, this is something that comes without toil. We have, however, seen dwellings of this sort constructed with old, yet good, shingles on the side walls which thus acquired at once the dignity of years. Again, as to the foliage, it is entirely feasible to secure a setting not only as good as this, but even superior. We remember journeying from Providence south on the Bristol side of the river, passing old sites, where the homesteads had burned, which were ideal so far as the surrounding elms and maples were concerned. We remember also seeing on the same drive a residence on which, it is said, a vast sum had been expended, but which was without a tree near it. The abrupt hills of Connecticut are more favorable for the formation of fine sites than we find elsewhere in New England. Furthermore their use is, for the most part, to be availed of, for the early homes were usually close to the highway and on valley roads. An old farm place may be used by making it the residence of a caretaker, and running an old lane

OLD HUGUENOT HOUSE — NEW LONDON

road to a higher ground where old oaks may provide a setting for a new
home, and the elevation may give an outlook. But who wants a large
dwelling when a small one is more beautiful? Only those who lack
imagination and observation.

The region about Mystic is alluring, owing to its numerous little walled-
in fields which look like play farms. They give an aspect of solidity to
a homestead. Probably there is no region in America that affords so
much of this particular sort of charm as that in the vicinity of Stonington. This district is a revelation even to a New Englander who has not
scanned it carefully.

In Newtown there is a great variety of scenery. There are lofty hills
with splendid outlooks which are not adapted for illustration, but are
amongst the airiest and noblest sites in the state, especially as one goes
toward Danbury. There are dells in the by-roads which, in favorable
seasons, yield such charms as appear on page 36 in Dell Blossoms. This
combination of water and blossom in Newtown has apparently escaped

BLOSSOM COVE—MANCHESTER

WATER WITCHERY—BROAD BROOK

BY THE MEADOW GATE—SOUTH BRITAIN

artists hitherto. If the author laid claim to be an artist, he certainly would do this scene in oils.

The Summer Grotto (page 36) is a bend in Broad Brook near Somers. Connecticut has not many wide stretches of lowlands and wherever the stream, as here, seeks its way doubtfully across a plain, turning here and there courteously to avoid any obstruction, as leisurely streams do since they have the time to cultivate good manners, the consequence is satisfactory to our esthetic sense. In fact we wonder whether, when we get weary of the swift highways, we shall not at length turn to the sinuous streams. On their placid surface alone does there seem to be time to stop, look and listen. The water ways are far more beautiful than the highways and are seldom frequented. We think there will always be room in the world to scan what is beautiful. We have never found crowds at view points that allured us. The best of the world is for people of quiet taste, for it is left neglected by the many. If we want harmony and silence and entrancing color and all that is best worth while, we shall find that there is very little competition for it. We are not among those that fear that the rich or the greedy or the subtle will gobble up the earth. As the crusty end of the French loaf is the best, and can always be had for the asking, so the loveliest flowers grow in the woodland, and the farther we proceed from the crowd the more desirable are the untouched surroundings.

Particularly there are in Connecticut large areas where, unmolested, we may make our own gardens, rear our own cottages, shape our own paths, and put the mark of our love and labor upon our intimate landscape. On a recent visit to California we were impressed by the evident purpose of many young couples to get into the country and dwell there. Possibly there will be a revival of the pioneer spirit to occupy the corners of New England which are nearer the great world, when we must go to it, and far more available to our means, than similar tracts in the great West. The plain of the Connecticut river is so thoroughly preëmpted,

[Continued on page 53]

BLOSSOM DALE

By Mildred Hobbs

Connecticut, the beautiful,
God made of you a paradise
Where glimpses of your cottage homes,
Through bowers of the birds, entice
My feet to wander down the trail
That leads to heaven in a dale.

In Eden was there such a nook —
A winding brook that purled about
Its blue-flagged isles, and then grew still —
And rainbow-flecked with darting trout?
And did its jewelled insects sail
On petal boats so fairy-frail?

Did apple blossoms blush as pink,
Or birds, sky-painted, sing like these
That flutter through the velvet depths
And stir the perfume of the trees?
Did green banks hide their grouse and quail
Beneath a sweeping flower-veil?

Low cottage windows from the hill
Look fondly down when Spring endows
Their slopes of paradise with song
Where nesting bluebirds sway the boughs
That bend to sweep the rustic rail
Along the path to Blossom Dale.

COTTAGE, BLOOM AND BROOK—NEWTOWN

UP THE PATH—WOODBURY

A FARMINGTON DOOR

A DUTCH COTTAGE—NORTH HAVEN

that people will at last awake to the fact that the smaller plains of its contributary streams are far more attractive. The smaller the valley the more beautiful, provided only one can look along it rather than across it. A local and individual growth is more attractive than a cosmopolitan character.

Brookside Blooms (page 39), found in Manchester, is a picture much loved. There is one perfect day in the year for catching the beauties of a particular spot. In some seasons even that day is lacking. There was never a wiser sentiment uttered by the wise man than this: that all things have their period of beauty, and that there is a time for everything. Doubtless there are hidden potentialities in the earth, awaiting, as they have waited for ages, their time of beauty. The Germans, in their search for war material, have incidentally brought to light the wonderful hidden colors that have slept so long in the coal measures. There is not a landscape on earth but will have its time of charm, and sometimes the charms last long, and seem to be as eternal as the spring.

The merit of making two blades of grass grow where one grew before is intended to refer, of course, purely to utilitarian matters. It is a

A SALEM GAMBREL

question whether the uses of beauty are not more to be cultivated in America, at the present time, than increased production of things to eat or wear. What higher appeal can nature make to us than that we assist her in making a little section of the world more beautiful? It is not necessary that the so called finished English landscape should cover all our acres. In fact, is a lawn, esthetically speaking, as beautiful as a pasture? A piece of velvet for a lady's gown is not as beautiful lying flat, as it is when draped in esthetic folds upon her person. We presume some Hollander may have been responsible, in the first place, for the erroneous notion that a perfectly level lawn is more attractive than a rolling ground. A deep seated prejudice in favor of lawns has resulted in the imitation, in an humble way, of the finished grass plot about English mansions. As a curve is more beautiful than a straight line, as applied to

ON BROAD BROOK   WOODBURY BLOSSOMS

STILL DEPTHS—SOUTH BRITAIN

AT WETHERSFIELD

highways, so it is when applied to the contour of the soil.

That portion of Connecticut, covered by the road from Manchester Center to the summit of Bolton Notch, affords Hartford an elevated region as a summer retreat. The railroad at the Notch is cut through a narrow slit. The east and west communications in Connecticut north of the shore have always been difficult, and hence has arisen the individual development of the various sections of the state, reminding us somewhat of the markedly distinctive features of various sections of England. Of course the flavor of these differences is now rapidly passing, since railways and motor roads have come in. There are, however, still some regions east of the Connecticut, in the highlands, where the old habits and speech and thought prevail, with very little change in two hundred and fifty years. The new highway from Glastonbury southeasterly will open a new life for a part of this region.

Dell Dale Road (page 40) is found as one tours out into the hills from Mystic. To our thought, the Spanish moss on southern oaks is not as beautiful as the vines that decorate our elms. The picture before us is much loved by the American people, although we do not know that it was brought to their attention until the author pictured it recently. When the touch of autumn has thrown its cast of reds and browns and yellows over the scene, the quiet rural sweetness of the spot is entrancing.

Homestead Blossoms (page 40) shows one of the square, so called salt box, houses so common in Connecticut. We have never been able to learn the significance of the name, as no salt box was ever made in this shape. Such, however, is the innate honesty of human nature that no one ever seems to challenge the appropriateness of the name.

The sketch on page 41, on the Woodbury-Southbury road, shows what is in autumn one of the fairest road scenes in Connecticut. The dwelling on the right has an old fashioned garden, and is set back in dignified grace from the highway. The next dwelling to it was the home of Peter Parley, a pen name that was a household word a generation since. This part of Connecticut between the hills of Middlebury and Newtown is distracting in its loveliness. There are other similar residences near charming old Woodbury.

The dwelling on page 45, with the gambreled L and the ordinary roof on the main house, with the old fashioned shed, all nestled beneath fine buttonwoods, is one of the attractive features as one goes from New Britain to Hartford. The buttonwood tree, never regular in its formation, always has a surprise for us in the way its branches spring forth. Their gnarled contour is decorative and artistic in a high degree.

The cottage on page 44, which we have named Bowered, is on the hills as one goes out of Waterbury towards Middlebury. It is a good example of the decorative effects of white lilac and apple blossoms, transforming a very ordinary little cottage into a delightsome retreat.

As one follows the old Boston Post Road from Norwalk toward Bridgeport, he will see on a side street, the little cottage on page 44 with the ribbon road winding through its gate. There is an eternal appeal in such individual driveways. They remind us of that greatest of all moments, that when we are nearing home after an absence. They are the more winning because they are devised purely with the thought of use, but inevitably sentiment gathers about them, as a vine clings to a tree. Sentiment is an element as important as paint in any picture.

Blossom Cove (page 47), on the river that skirts the highway between Manchester and Hartford, is a picture much loved. It is, happily, in the time of high water in spring, when the blossoms are out, that it is available, and is one more instance of the principle already mentioned that there is only a day in the year, only one time that is perfect for anything of this sort.

There are other scenes along this stream fully as beautiful.

On page 46 is a sketch of the old Huguenot House, New London. It stands surrounded with modern dwellings, a relic of the earlier times. Its excellent stone end, of which the chimney is only a projection, is further enhanced in attractiveness by vine growth. Happily the little

SLACK WATER—WOODBURY

AN OLD BACK DOOR

WOODBURY BANKS

A WILTON HOMESTEAD

picket fence has been retained around the front. The dwelling is maintained as a tea house and has, in addition, some early curiosities.

New London is rather notable for its quaint surroundings, attractive drives and nearby resorts. Take it for all in all, it may perhaps be counted the most important shore center between Boston and New York. It is just large enough as a strolling ground for the traveler. It is so old and so individual as to vie with Hartford and New Haven and Saybrook, forming with them a fourth ancient state center. It also forms the gate through which one turns northerly to Worcester and northwesterly to Hartford. It shares with other Connecticut towns that local pride which induces the erection of dignified public edifices and will, in time, render all such towns architecturally attractive.

Water Witchery on Broad Brook (page 48) is another of those winning compositions with which nature gratuitously provides us. The very slight ripple, merely a wrinkle of water, on sands, constitutes an element in composition of no small importance. It is often necessary for artistic effects to break up the water, thus avoiding duplications and that doubled picture effect, which the novice imagines desirable. It is a curious fact that water, breaking in this herring-bone fashion, may be pictured by a time exposure without a trace of motion. The formation of the ripple remains

AN INTERESTING SIGN—OLD SAYBROOK

continuously the same. That is important, as in dark compositions time
is often necessary.

By the Meadow Gate (page 48) is a familiar scene. The nearness
of the blossoming tree to the gate, adds that charm to country
occupations which is too often deplorably lacking in mechanical trades.
Nature herself always strives to be beautiful, however some persons may
deny the fact. The farmer has a love, possibly unconscious, for the setting which is given to his home and his field roads, by his orchards and
shade trees. He is more likely to respond to the call of beauty than is
the mechanic. The mere fact that he dwells by preference in the country,
at the present time, when there is a very strong pull citywards, is a mark
of a good deal of character. The writers on political economy sometimes
fail to give the farmer credit for remaining on the farm. In the ancient
day, the farmer took up mechanical work in the winter. Then he did
on his tools and racks what is now done in shops. In the spring he perhaps sawed his own lumber. He was thus able to vary his work. Even
now he sometimes enters a manufacturing plant during the slack season
of farm work. It is well recognized, however, by the farmer as well as

MEADOW BLOSSOMS — MANCHESTER

WE'RE YOUNG — SOUTHBURY

OVERHANG HOUSE — FARMINGTON

by the student of economics that farm work is less productive, financially, than various other occupations in which the farmer might engage. We are, therefore, bound to conclude that it is largely a matter of taste with the farmer that he remains on his land. Partly, indeed, he may enjoy the independence thus secured. But largely we are glad to believe he has a love for growing things and the harmonies of nature. His home naturally means more to him than any city home could mean, because it is not merely a dwelling, but it is placed in the midst of surroundings as distinctive as the edifice itself. Besides the home sense which, in the city dweller, must gather around his residence only, the farmer feels the added objects of affection supplied by "the orchard, the meadow, the deep tangled wildwood." His home out of doors is as distinctive, and more winning, than his home indoors. In short, it requires character to live in the country, but none to live in town. The man who exists merely for money-making, and the man lacking initiative, are found in the country only as sporadic exceptions.

Woodbury is an attractive old town. Its little Masonic Temple perched on a cliff is a curiosity much thought of, especially amongst the brotherhood. There is a fine cliff back of the town, the summit of which has been reserved for a local park. The long drive through Woodbury and Southbury is almost a continuous village for many miles, but of so open a character that most of the residences stand in large plots. The Chinese laundryman complained that it was too much longee and too little widee! A bright and cultivated lady was asked if she did not feel the want of congenial society in this region. She replied, " Oh, well, the street is long." The philosophy in this remark is capable of wide extension. If the next door neighbor and even the next again does not appeal to us, we shall find someone who does on the long street. We do not, of course, intend to hint that people are rare in Woodbury who are worth knowing, because we have learned to the contrary.

Up the Path (page 52) is along a stream in Woodbury. A Farmington Door (page 52) is just a glimpse of that super-village, with the best possible school, and spire, and quaint dwellings — all situated at the ideal distance from Hartford. Farmington is unique as containing more framed overhang houses than any other town in the new world.

From North Woodbury to Watertown is a winding drive over sightly hills past interesting homesteads. Watertown, on its upper streets, affords many beautiful village compositions. The town further has the advantage of the Taft school, which imparts an intellectual tone to the village. A New England village which is made the home of an endowed academy and has, in addition, a good old church edifice or two and a few early homes, all located in the hill country with pleasing outlook, makes a powerful appeal to those who love at once a rural neighborhood and scholastic atmosphere.

Passing through Watertown to Plymouth, the fertile mother of so many mechanical inventions, we may go on the old road to Hartford through Terryville.

THE CRAB APPLE—SOUTHBURY

HOUSATONIC SHADOWS

THE MILL, A. D. 1653 — NEW LONDON

WOLCOTT HOMESTEAD — LITCHFIELD

The three old towns, Wethersfield, Hartford and Windsor, as colonial history has told us, form the heart of the state of Connecticut. These townships spread out over great areas in which other towns have since been carved out. They included, in fact, the cream of the finest Connecticut river lands; and at a very early period reached a development and a cultivation, both of persons and acres, which set a high mark for the rest of the state to attain to. Traveling overland from Massachusetts Bay, the settler's colony secured a peculiar preëminence in this respect: it was composed of the deeply cut religious characteristics of the Puritans, and it settled upon lands of great fertility. We have here, therefore, a unique community, or a community rivalled by Springfield alone. That is, only in these instances do we find the juxtaposition of the exile for conscience, and the environment of fertile acres in a considerable community. The consequence was that the growth of this three-town colony proceeded on lines rather different from those of other New England communities. These three towns constituted an independent state and, with their cherished charter and their fine location, they proceeded to work out, with some natural errors, a theory of society untrammeled by the past, except as that lived in them. Architecturally they built dwellings and furniture of a type found nowhere else in America. The type was marked by what we may call a sturdy, yet aesthetic ideal. As a political body the community recorded itself with peculiar laws, most of which were found wise, and even those which were otherwise, indicated a powerful set of mind toward what the settlers regarded as an ideal society. We have not credited such communities with the advantage which they have offered to the nation at large in the development of its law making, and its social ideas. The Hartford colony tried out certain experiments in a new land, so that we can see how they worked and whether they are feasible.

We are particularly indebted, very deeply, to the combination in these settlers of sturdy religious character combined with mechanical capacity and a powerful home love. They built there dwellings of oak even to the clapboards. They cut their mortises deep and pinned them for the

DWELLING WITH OVERHANG—COLCHESTER

ages, so that a cross section of a Connecticut house frame is no poor exhibit of the moral character of the people who made it.   Hartford,
indeed, in its years of recent growth, forgot the signal merit of those
dwellings, and swept them away; but Wethersfield and Windsor have still
preserved many of them, with their noble doorheads, their long lean-tos,
their ample proportions, and the unmistakable marks of character combined with good taste, a possibly rare but certainly delightful coalescence.

The river was their broad and excellent channel of communication with
each other.   In those days shipping was conveniently carried on with
vessels of comparatively shallow draft.   The settler's lands, inundated
in the spring like Egypt, took toll from the sediment of the river at
least over a section of their meadows, and their fertile acres became the
first and, perhaps, still remain the first specialized garden spots of America.
Hartford as a trade center became also, therefore, the source of the finer
articles of household furnishings which were transported to the new residences in adjoining valleys, and away up the Connecticut into southern

BETWEEN THE BLOSSOMS—LONG HILL ROAD

THE GOLDEN WEST—LITCHFIELD COUNTY

GOING TO WORK—SANDY HOOK

WHO'S IN THE PARLOR?—WOODBURY

THOMAS LEE HOUSE—EAST LYME

New Hampshire and Vermont. One of the best pieces of carving in this country, showing as it does the traditions of sixteenth century work in the round, was found in Lyme, New Hampshire, and was doubtless carried up the Connecticut river. The city of Hartford became the center of cabinet work in the seventeenth century. Some specimens remain of carved wainscotting as well as of doorhead and hall decorations. For this specialized mechanical ability of the Connecticut valley, centering at Hartford, developed and maintained its supremacy as it does today. The dwellings erected in this region in the eighteenth century were of a very excellent character. The magnificent oaks, which are so marked a feature of Connecticut scenery, once abounded in vast numbers and they stand yet as a symbol of her people. It is not an accident that the charter and the oak are indissolubly connected. A dwelling of oak beneath an oak tree, with mighty arms of protection reaching out over it, is a fine and satisfactory nucleus around which our thought of the best elements of the past may gather. It is true the oak was often gnarled and so were the people. They were a strong, sometimes even crabbed or cantankerous sort, but they lasted. They had the idea of eternity planted in their souls. When they were right they were magnificent. The tree that grows in the open has the biggest knots, but it is also the strongest. The bark of the oak clings closely. Some of these settlers were a little close. If they had not been, they would not have preserved for us the works of their fathers, and America would have been vastly poorer without the background of the Connecticut handiwork and traditions. They worked for what they got, and they kept it. We are not sure that when truly worthy appeals came to those people, that they lacked any degree of that bigness of soul which marks American character. For, in spite of what European brethren say, generosity is probably the most marked feature of the American people, if we are restricted to naming only one. The Hartford colony is a rather notable example, almost an embodiment, of the axiom — to prove all things and to hold fast that which is good. Take it for all in all, it is this American colony which, even more than Plymouth which was very small and Boston Bay which was more mixed, is the most striking individual example of an American colony of remarkable and individual character.

There is ever a kind of coquettishness about an old house. It beckons us to know what hidden charms it contains. The Wilton Homestead (on page 61) has slowed many a motor, and with good warrant. For the massiveness of its old kitchen chimney and the rambling passages of its ell are worth inspection. More than one good old specimen of early day furnishing may have passed from the fine old dwelling, though some good examples still remain.

The back doors of old houses are more interesting than the front doors, especially when, as on page 60, the dry stone wall supplied a foundation for the steps, and flowers and vines and trees completed the setting. Little paradises are often feasible at back doors. The homely outlines are

BLOSSOM BEND — TALCOTTVILLE

WHERE GRANDMA WAS WED — LITCHFIELD COUNTY

A ROADSIDE APPLE TREE—OXFORD

POMFRET WATERS

A GABLE AT GROTON

a temptation to decorate with those fruits or furnishings that concern the intimate life. A Dutch love for the bright dairy dishes hung to air at the back door, is not a matter to be overlooked in an effort at simple truth. The bed of mint, the clump of mustard, the stalks of milkweed, all help to furnish forth the table and are as near and useful as possible. The cherry tree with white blossom or crimson fruit crowns all. The back door is the setting also of the family council at the end of day in summer time, with the cosset lamb and the hen with her brood circling about. An old back door has more of humanity in it than any other part of the homestead.

It is there that farm plans are made, and the fields are considered, one by one, as their capacity to add to the farmer's income is reckoned. It is there that hopes of the growing family are cherished, and careers are sketched. There the housewife with her apron and her bare, capable arms sits, her man at her knee, and her children clustering about. It is all a court of the common people.

There is something almost impertinent in the blossoming of an ancient apple tree (page 63). Its main limbs broken, its trunk sapped by suckers, its interior full of squirrel paths, it looks in early spring about the most useless, unsightly thing above ground. But with opening May, the ascending sap opens its buds again, and it blandly stands forth in a new enrapturing gown of pale pink and exclaims: " We're young! deny it if you dare! " Indeed many an old trunk, overthrown by a heavy spring blast, will blossom even when prostrate, provided some little slivers still connect it with the stump. It is easy to discourage a young tree, but not an old one. There are usually offered at least a few apples to convince us that life is good and sound, and that it pays to try. By its zigzag rail fence it endeavors to bring a tribute of beauty, as ground rent.

The dwelling on page 65 is the only one of the sort, that we know in America, having a satisfactory location. On strongly rising ground overlooking the Farmington valley, and with generous freedom from the intrusion of other dwellings, it forms a most delightful feature. Good trees are about it, an old well curb is gratefully near one corner. It is at the edge of the village, as any ideal homestead must be. Happy the hand that has held it from destruction, and kept it to flavor our day with the quaintness, the romance, the sturdiness and the love of good decora-

THE UNBROKEN FLOW—POMPERAUG RIVER

A SIP OF TEA—SOUTHBURY

RIBBON LANE—BRANCHVILLE

GOLDEN AUTUMN—SHELTON

tion, which must again spring up in the American character if we are to reap the benefits of our heredity and our environment.

Elm Drapery (page 64), on the road to Bridgewater, shows what trees will do for us, when we allow them to try. There are no more perfect curves than those assumed by elm branches. Their sweep varies widely in different specimens, but it is always symmetrical. The apple has none of this peculiar grace, but gives us color and fruit, while the elm offers us decoration in form.

The crabapple blossoms somewhat earlier than other apples (page 67). The cherry tree in New England is the first field tree to usher in the spring. The magnolia is a trifle earlier than either, but as the magnolia seems to be the special pet of the wealthy, we have never caught an example of it in picturesque connection with the cottage home.

Some of the old roads on the Housatonic used to yield pleasant shadowy stretches before the great dam filled the stream and overflowed. Such scenes as on page 67 show that this occurence has not been without compensations. More beautiful shore lines have been formed than those that were destroyed, and projects of other dams may add no little to the beauties of this part of Connecticut through Southbury and Newtown and thence to the north. The somewhat wild and narrow valley has not been important enough, in an agricultural sense, to call for anything more than narrow, ancient roads.

It is told that the burning of an early Southbury church started an equally fiery discussion regarding the location of the new edifice. Some said that the building must be placed north of a certain oak tree. Others insisted the new church should be erected to the south of that oak. The southern end of the parish carried the day, and the northern faction refused to attend church; but when another sect of Christians built still farther south, the disgruntled, going directly past the new edifice of their brethren, threw in their lot with the later comers! Such is our human nature. We are at least comforted by the reflection that our ancestors had enough religion to fight over. Into this village,

A COS COB DOOR

now too small for one good church, a third sect came and built.
A few years since, there was worship in none of the three, except spas-
modically, and the village had no resident pastor. One might conclude

A MEMORY OF CHILDHOOD—SIMSBURY

A HINT OF SEPTEMBER—WOODBURY

WALLINGFORD STREET

HOUSATONIC BROADS

MIDDLE HADDAM LIBRARY

that non-conformity is the great curse of old country towns. But such is not the case. Pretty generally the people go nowhere to church, and scarcely do they meet to vote. Despite the spread of newspapers there is no small contingent of the population without the stimulus of public opinion, and who fall back on their own narrow interpretation of life. They are shrewd traders. They must be, or starve. Some have a small patrimony of two or three thousand dollars, which supplies a little sum of ready money as interest. With this meager fund they buy a few necessities and hibernate. It is not a pleasing prospect. It is the opposite of the immigration question. The delinquent or moribund old English stock of course dies out or wakes up. But it is hard to face the simple truth: Where the grandfathers of such people filled the churches and cultivated

[Continued on page 89]

STILL WATERS

By Mildred Hobbs

" He leadeth me beside the still waters,
  He restoreth my soul."

Where trees bend down their beauty to the stream,
Full-foliaged their painted shadows lie
Upon the tinted mirror of the sky,
Where dawns reflect and flames of sunset gleam.
And lilies, ferns, and fringing grasses seem
To contemplate their faces, and to vie
With all the meadow's charms that glorify
The day — and here I walk with God, and dream.

Away from tumults of the world's unrest,
The sad confusion of its cults and creeds,
Awaits a manifested Love and Might
To shame the wrangling and the fevered quest.
Beside still waters God's great presence leads
And fills my soul with faith and peace and light.

THE COTTAGE ON THE FLOSS—OXFORD

A LITTLE PENINSULAR—MANCHESTER

LIGHT ON A DARK SUBJECT

A SOUTHBURY BARNYARD

their acres diligently and reared large families, educating them for a large Americanism, where they had fine homes and intelligent self-respect, this generation stagnates and, industrially, politically and religiously, is a feeble reflection of the third generation before it.

The remarkably notable mill on page 68, has been briefly alluded to, but we cannot refrain from the expression of delight we feel in an American manufacturing institution which is said to have been continuously at work since 1653, an exceptional, if not a unique, record. The quaintness of this structure is equal to its age.

The Wolcott Homestead (page 68) is only one of many in Litchfield to hold the eye of the explorer. Many of these quaint dwellings are rich in memorials of the past, and others are being enriched by the zeal of the collectors who dwell in them.

One gentleman of our acquaintance, recently married, is an ardent collector of early Americana. He would not have a new thing in his house if he knew it. On the occasion of the coming of his first born, a son, a friend wrote him expressing surprise to hear that he had gone in for reproductions. Our friend replied that at any rate the piece concerned was native American, and a bandy-legged low-boy with bawl and claw!

The region just north of Litchfield is not as interesting as that east, west and south. Litchfield has this advantage, that it is the terminus of a railway branch, and free of the noise of through traffic; is high, quiet, dignified, stately. A fine recruiting ground for the nerves and far from our rushing modern life. Its traditions, its situation, its architectural features, its mellowed society are all contributory to its charm. There is something steady about the Connecticut spirit, comparable, in this country, only with that of Pennsylvania. You must show a Connecticut man a better way before he will relinquish his old way. And you must make a good case. If there is a loophole in your argument he will find it. When you have finally established, beyond cavil, that you are right, and have perhaps secured an admission of the fact, and begin to look for action, you are floored by the quiet remark that the old way after all is very good, and that custom has made it comfortable, and therefore, there will be no change. In short, the Connecticut man likes his way, and will stick to it, accomplishing more, sometimes, than he could by changing to what seems better now. He has seen people coming back to the old ways after abandoning them for a hundred years; so, who knows, he may be in the height of fashion soon, or, if not, his son or grandson will be. The methods of education pass around their whirligig and come back whence they started. He has noted the shift of human thought and the fads of successive generations, but he finds himself even now as well fitted to meet the world as those who have ever been shifting. If we wait long enough we shall eventually be right.

In these remarks we are referring to the better class of old-time Connecticut citizens. Of course, there are always those who put new jim-cracks on old dwellings and make amendments to the ten commandments. There are plenty of people who are so broad that they are shallow.

The Long Hill Road from Bridgeport to Danbury through Newtown opens a broad country to view and spreads forth its fields and orchards in appealing fashion. The streams of New Haven County are as attractive as one can find anywhere. The drive from Waterbury southerly shows many a bold hill handsomely mirrored in a reservoir of the Naugatuck. This valley has been rich in contributing many inventions now of universal application. Every little village has produced its mechanical genius, and every large town has furnished scores of men to set in motion the vast industries of the west. If a tally were made of the great industrial centers of Ohio and Michigan it would be found that the basic principles of the work done there were thought out to a surprising degree by Connecticut men, or their sons.

We do not recollect whether anyone has elaborated the relation between poor soil and inventive genius. But if necessity be the mother of invention, many interesting illustrations of the fact may be found in Connecticut. Where the acres were meager and poor and shut in between hills forbidding agriculture, men's minds naturally turned in other directions

A LANE IN NORWICHTOWN

EARLY SUMMER — POMPERAUG RIVER

ON THE WAY TO COLD SPRING

A SUMMER DREAM—LITCHFIELD COUNTY

A CONNECTICUT GATEWAY

than cultivating the soil. Among fertile acres the inhabitants are intent on their lands. It will be interesting for someone to trace out the debt of the world to poor soils. In the barren hills where a railway passes, one sees in Massachusetts a toppling sign: " Elias Howe, inventor of the sewing machine was born in this town."

The glebe house, Woodbury, is said to be the earliest Episcopalian rector's residence. In those days a house with field attached was sometimes a part of the clergyman's compensation. This particular dwelling has connected with it a tale amusing now but serious enough at the time. The rector being attached to the English church was naturally a Tory. He spoke his sentiments quite openly on Sunday, to the wrath of the revolutionaries. Yet such was the sentiment, or the law, that a clergyman could not be molested on Sunday, any more than a legislator could be taken from the State House. When on Monday the authorities sought to find their man they failed. It was afterwards told that he was hidden in a secret chamber of the chimney, and a woodbox heaped high was placed at the orifice of his hiding place. At safe intervals the clergyman came out. The game was kept up for some time. It is believed that the chased parson ultimately escaped, but this is not a history. We merely show a quaint nearby house (page 72). It is to be hoped that the human habit, in history, of relating almost nothing of the human side, may by this time have been overcome.

The valley of the Pomperaug, where Woodbury is situated, lies back of Sherman Hill, one of the specially steep state roads, almost prohibitory before the days of the automobile.

Much has been made by artists of farm scenes, showing the workers engaged in their labors on the land. These pictures always have interest to those who like people. Not enough has been done of this sort in America, though the New England hay rack, the Conestoga wagon of Pennsylvania, the prairie schooner, the plowing scenes and many other phases of farm life are worthy of record. Such pictures may be more difficult, but they are very attractive when well done.

" Going to Work " (page 72) shows, behind, the typical old red house with its stone chimney, once so common in Connecticut and even now not rare.

It is often difficult, in such themes as " Blossom Bend " (page 75), to secure apple blossoms at the same time with foliage on the maples, elms and buttonwoods. Nature is a little freakish, and sometimes an elm, being somewhat out of health, will be quite bare when the apple trees are in full flower.

The old dwelling, " Where Grandma Was Wed " (page 75), seems very appealing, with its buttonwoods to the left, its great maple in front, and apple trees on either hand. One longs to know the story of the generations who dwelt here. For many years the house has been forsaken and is now falling in. A very little care would have preserved it. It was a notion exploded long since that people may be trusted by self-interest, to preserve their own property. The succession of abandoned

THE ROAD OR THE BYWAY?—LITCHFIELD COUNTY

AUGUST IN THE MEADOWS—LITCHFIELD COUNTY

AMONG THE LITCHFIELD HILLS

A LITCHFIELD STREET

homes one passes in touring a state is another proof that the best things are the least cared for. The American family refuses these days to live far from a market. But this old dwelling was only three miles from a large village, reached by a level road. We remember a door with the remarkable number of seven bull's-eye panes in the transom over it. The owners had abandoned the house and lived near by. But they will not sell the sash. Year by year some vandal knocked out one after another of the bull's eyes, on the principle in vogue among boys that, if a thing is going, they should help it along. Now the glass is all gone. Some of the finest paneling and the most beautiful door heads have similarly gone the way of all the earth. The owner of one dwelling would never sell though he had removed elsewhere. Finally the house was wrecked and given away for fire wood with no effort to dispose of it!

France would live and thrive on the waste products of America. It is partly in the hope of encouraging at least a few persons to maintain the best of the past, that these volumes are being put forth. Another purpose is to retain a record of that which is passing away, so that we may have a truer conception than a literary description alone could give. A pictorial history is both more accurate and more rare and is more readily understood than is any other sort.

Among the most beautiful districts in Connecticut are those in the northeastern part. The land is high with long, sweeping hills and fine prospects. Pomfret, Brooklyn, Woodstock and Putnam are largely occupied by ideal farms. There is a splendid sense of strength and freedom on these fertile, high slopes. Pomfret has become fashionable, and the other towns mentioned are also being sought. Pomfret Waters (page 76) is a pool in a private estate. Pomfret street is a stately thoroughfare, but Brooklyn village is more of an earlier type. It has been reckoned among the half dozen most attractive American villages.

One has the sense of being in a wide and independent domain when on a hill farm with much open land. There is scarcely any other sensation comparable with this. On a great mountain one looks upon barrens. The sense of possession and breadth and plenty combined with the wide prospect are amongst the greatest joys given to man.

In the harmonizing of city and country taste, in adapting country seats, there is sometimes an incongruous overlapping. After careful study, one is inclined to say that if the estate is so far made prim as to indicate the hand of the city owner plainly, a little too much has been done. The walls, while they should be made good, ought never to be laid in cement, as that was not done by the farmers. They sometimes did erect solid double walls that stood for generations. Such a wall does not lack harmony with the landscape, whereas a masonry wall in the country field has the tendency to cause us to raise our eyebrows. The same rule applies to the building. A little too much in the way of decoration spoils all. Country places were never decorated so as to take away the attention from their substantial principal outlines. Thus a shingled barn is more convincing than one that is clapboarded, though clapboards were used sometimes by the farmers. Iron gates at once say to us, " This is not a farm but a place where money is sported." On the dwelling itself there is often too much in the way of a flamboyant porch, such as at once proclaims itself as built to be looked at. When there are many well educated architects who have not yet learned the principle of restraint, of course it is to be expected that city people who have come into the possession of ample means, but who have not had a training in esthetics or architecture, should overdo their constructions. Often some little thing about a dwelling is enough to destroy the sense of farm values. A good question to ask oneself is this: " What could a thrifty farmer have afforded? "

It requires the greatest care to compare every little added feature with similar features in good old country places. If we find them nowhere in legitimate farm houses, we ought not to add them when we restore or enlarge. A purchaser who begins to improve his place may say, as he often does, " This is my place and I can do what I wish with it." Does he ask what is the motive of his expenditures? If it is merely to indicate that a good deal has been spent, then we have nothing further to say,

WATERS MEET — POMPERAUG RIVER

CLOUDS OVER THE HOUSATONIC

A CANAAN PASTURE

FIELD LANE—WINDHAM COUNTY

because the owner has put himself avowedly outside the bounds of taste. If, however, the question arises, what is an ideal farmhouse, we have a substantial basis of procedure, which, if strictly adhered to, may result in a very charming series of farm buildings. On the other hand some may say that they are not spending money just to show it, but rather because they want all the amplitude of city comforts in the country. The fallacy here, is that these comforts are supposed not to be obtainable in a large farmhouse. As a matter of fact, every comfort and luxury may be contained within the ample space of a legitimate farmhouse. It is a nice question which has been solved in some instances very successfully. Some things to be avoided are too great height in buildings, every sort of superfluous decoration and any walk with a cut margin of turf.

It has always been a mystery that people grow so ecstatic about autumn foliage but seem to care very little for autumn farm scenes connected with the gathering in of the harvest. The shocks of corn or grain and the yellow pumpkins, backed by fine trees or water, make a composition which is lacking in no artistic element, and in no appeal to sentiment. In some states like Pennsylvania a fad is made of farming operations carried on just as they used to be. The city dweller limits himself to the setting and the method of the farmers around him and, in this respect, he is in the right. In many cases the fad is forgotten and a pure love of the agricultural aspects of the country is developed.

What can be more alluring, more appealing to the feeling and the esthetic sense, than a ribbon lane leading up to one's own dwelling set in the midst of the home acres? Suppose now, one was to cut away the ribbons of turf, to fill this drive with colored gravel, and prepare a precise margin. The charm would be utterly lost. Yet there are many thousands of such places where vast sums are squandered. Have those responsible for the imitation of ducal estates in England asked themselves what they are really doing? Their edifices are not ducal. Their approaches are short as compared with the great landed estates. At best, the result is a poor imitation. If we are just willing to take country beauties as we find them, merely pruning and banishing rubbish, we often achieve a result thoroughly satisfactory. In Pennsylvania they build new post and rail fences to harmonize with the usual fence of the country roads. If we likewise imitate our good old wall we shall be nearer the mark so far as harmony, beauty and good taste are concerned.

The harmonizing of improvements on a country place is a very special branch of architecture combined with landscape gardening. The landscapist of fifty years ago felt himself under obligation to reproduce so far as possible a European model. Now he knows that, if he consults the local requirements very carefully, he reaches results far more desirable. Nor can he work alone. The architect must be ready to meet him, not by offering some monument to his own skill, but by pruning and adapting and toning his work to the attractive simplicity of the neighborhood.

There is another criterion of success, in combing out a country farm. Let the question constantly be asked, is my scheme pictorial? If it will not compose as an attractive, artistic unity, something too much or too little has been done. All marks of recent newness must be avoided, as well as slovenliness. A nice middle course is required. If the result makes a good picture, then nothing has been done that ought not to have been done. If an artist says, this spick and span fence or gable should not have been here, then the blended effect is lost, and the object of producing just what one loves to see has not been attained.

The fine relic on page 65 of an American framed overhang house, has probably the best situation of any such dwelling in America, as it is on a quiet upper street in Farmington and pretty well removed from the street. The saddest feature connected with our early American dwellings is that, for the most part, they are in unsightly places, or huddled against the highway. The writer does not remember a half a dozen seventeenth century houses in a good setting. All the more, when such an example is found, it is the interest of the whole body of citizens to foster its preservation and to allow it to suggest the lines of development in its vicinity.

At the corner of this dwelling there is an old well with a windlass.

ON THE QUINNEBAUG

THE GREETING

THE WATERS OF CANAAN

We have never been much taken with the well sweep, as it seems more or less ungainly. The windlass well is susceptible of various styles of legitimate treatment, all of which are charming and reminiscent of the old days.

On page 83 is that effect which we always hail with delight, an apple blossom so situated that it makes a frame for a cottage. Under the over-reaching branch appear the roof lines. The esthetic position is always one which thus reveals a part of a dwelling. Sometimes it seems necessary to show the entire bare outlines, but if a portion of them can, as in this instance, be masked in blossom, we are so much the better satisfied.

It may be worth while to suggest how the attraction of a dwelling is enhanced by viewing it beneath a noble tree. As one wanders through Connecticut there are many old sites where dwellings have been burned, which may be treated so as to procure this effect.

On page 84, Wallington Street has fine rows of elms leading down to the Choate School, which give an atmosphere to this village ridge in the midst of the plain. The village is the first, as one moves north from the shore about New Haven, that appeals to us. Obviously the location has been appraised at its proper worth, for the village is thriving and growing.

The red soil in this portion of Connecticut, rising from the disintegra-tion of the once fashionable brown stone, contributes a warming and cheering effect to the spring landscape, quite in contrast with the cold blue clay districts in Maine. While we do not for a moment imagine that country places are chosen on account of the color of the soil, nevertheless the writer remembers with a shudder looking out as a child upon bare, ploughed fields of blue-white clay.

The shale or trap rock of some portions of western Connecticut forms wonderfully attractive contours on the hills and is a perfect natural road material requiring no preparation.

To connect a bridge with a cottage, as is done on page 87, is to achieve a good deal in the way of landscape adornment; though an ideal arrange-ment would be a winding or diagonal approach. The premises concerned

A COTTAGE IN WILLIMANTIC

have been, in past years, a good deal neglected and overgrown; but with a little care the setting could be rendered wonderfully pleasing.

How far we have marched from the past, sometimes appears in the old pamphlets dug out from the garret, as one on page 88 entitled "Light on a Dark Subject."

It is somewhat saddening to reflect that practically all discussions on religion have left thinkers precisely in the position they occupied in the beginning. An hundred years ago and more it was the intellectual exercise of our ancestors to debate. They learned to be better talkers by the process, but whether they were spiritually uplifted we may doubt.

A Southbury Barnyard (page 88) with the hay coming down from the loft into the generous manger, and the eager appetite of the sheep, must ever pull at the heart strings of any man who was born on a farm. There is something about a flock of sheep which appeals to a very ancient sense in man, as our adjective *pecuniary* comes direct from the flock, indicating

CANAAN CURVES

WHERE THE COWS GO HOME — LITCHFIELD

SHADOW OF THE BLOSSOMS—LITCHFIELD COUNTY

GRANDMOTHER'S SHEFFIELD—WETHERSFIELD

that a sheep was an ancient and perhaps the original object of barter and standard of value before coins were struck.

There is engrained in our constitution the sense of being at home when we are amongst sheep. They were the companions and the property of man, even before he owned land. While he was a wanderer on the face of the earth, and had no fixed habitation, and built no dwelling.

To the feminine mind there always seems an incongruity in sending away for slaughter the sheep which one has tended for a decade. In the old days this incongruity was sought to be remedied in part by giving a cosset to the children and even to the mother. But even so, the closer personal relationship between the pet and the owner only deepened the pang of a final necessary separation. The meeting of the angels with Abraham brings to our mind the pathetic surprise of the calf that was caught to furnish forth the feast. These strange inconsistencies in life are more emphasized in the country than in the towns. We believe, however, that the farmer is more tender hearted than those who do not have immediately to do with animals. He is careful to make short work of their pain, at last. We are reminded that humane and enlightened men are deliberating whether or not we humans also would not be better for some custom of quickly and quietly putting us out of the way, when we become a burden to ourselves and to those we love. We have in mind various instances where a faithful old horse has been pastured and maintained free of care for years, only to be put out of the way at last. It is sometimes a question where mercy lies. We shall never forget the pathetic chloroforming of a domestic animal, when the owner was to remove far from the possibility of its care.

Gateways of country places are well worthy of a volume of their own. While the variety is very great, a simple sort as on page 93, which is attractive indeed, is rare, although it should not be. Here we have two huge stone posts, and a gate of heavy slabs bolted to stringers. It is found in Stamford. In preparing a gateway, two objects, as always, should be kept in mind, beauty and strength, and one is impossible without the other. That is to say, a flimsy gate, no matter how elaborate, proclaims its weakness, so that we cannot think of it as beautiful. One of the commonest and saddest sights on a country road is a massive cut stone gateway, the dwelling behind which is either burned or neglected. It is not a credit to human mentality that so much trouble and expense should be given to cut stone posts when stones not cut, like those above, are so very much more attractive. The French farmhouse system spans the gatepost with a huge lintel which is often thatched to prevent disintegration or decay. It must be lofty enough to admit a hay wagon. The French gate suggests in some degree a Chinese gate, which is spanned in a similar manner and, of course, for the same purpose originally. Without such a spanning member it is difficult, without massive construction, to erect posts which will bear the continual strain of a pull in one direction. But even so, deeply set, well tamped, heavy posts will stand.

A Lane in Norwichtown (page 91) answers all our craving in the way of country beauty, with its ribbon road and stone wall, its mysterious distance and its wealth of bloom. Norwichtown is somewhat rich in attractive scenes.

On the Way to Cold Spring (page 92) is a drive westerly from Danbury, with that endless attraction of dancing shadows and half lights seen in the sunlight through a woodland.

Reverting to the discussion of gateways just above, a few rules may be laid down as of general application:

1. The solidest and most massive material available should be used. For this purpose nothing is so satisfactory as a monolith. Stonehenge pillars make fine gateways as, indeed, they were doubtless intended to do. There are very few districts in New England where a natural stone is not available for hinging a gate. If such a stone cannot be found, it is readily broken out from a surface ledge. It can never be too large, and if it has

SKIRTING THE POOL—E. WINDSOR HILL

AN INSPIRATION—WETHERSFIELD

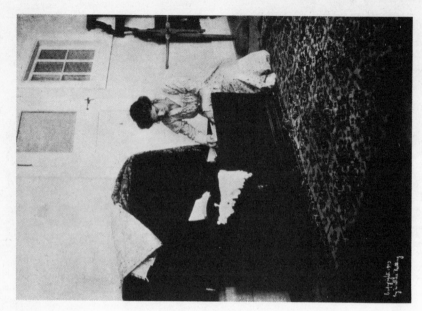

RUMMAGING IN THE ATTIC

CHILDISH REFLECTIONS

one side which may be made approximately vertical, that is all that is required.

2. Brick for gateways should be avoided if possible, as it tends to disintegrate with the strain placed upon it, and with the liability of collision.

3. The next best material to natural stone is cement, which should be constructed with reinforcements, made rather simple in outline and crested so as to shed water. Such posts should be set five feet in the ground, and ought not to be less than two feet square.

4. From a previous statement it will be seen that wood is never necessary. If, however, its use is insisted upon, the best variety is locust and, failing that, cedar. If posts of either of these woods are peeled, and left otherwise in the rough, and made with cone tops painted on the peak, and set deeply enough, being composed of massive timbers, they will perhaps last for one or two generations.

5. A very attractive post may be a living tree in which huge gudgeons may be fixed to sustain the gate. Such use may not injure the tree at all and the effect is pleasing, as is always the case whenever we can adapt our wants so as to work directly with nature.

6. We feel strongly that the gate with the cross member subtending the two posts, is the most permanent and attractive method of construction, if wood is used. The cross section should be chamfered each way on the top, and should extend a foot or so beyond the post, finishing in a molded curve, and being framed with the post. This cross member affords a good space for inscribing the name of the country place which may be done with sections of cedar saplings, to form the letters.

7. All patent gates should be avoided as none have ever been constructed of sufficiently substantial materials. Anybody can make a better gate than can be purchased.

But after our gate is thus constructed, we may as well ask what no one ever seems to ask beforehand, what is the purpose of the gate? Certainly it is not designed to be used. Not once in a myriad of times do we find the gate of a country place closed, and even if it is so, one can generally find a rear approach that is open. Apparently, this truth has dawned on some who have erected fine posts but have omitted the gate. An excellent compromise may be suggested in the way of a couple of chains hooked across the opening, provided one wishes to keep out stray animals or to indicate that the latch string is not out. Of course these chains would not be used after the first week of their installation.

If one, however, insists upon erecting a gate, one should also prepare a lodge and employ a porter, a custom more and more going out in these days, when there is always more useful work that can be done. In England, the porter's wife or child sometimes attends the gate. In America, the employment of a porter always seems a bit snobbish, except in the case of those few magnificent estates where the owner is in danger of being bothered by the curious.

If a gate is used, beautiful iron grill work may constitute an attractive feature. Such gates in many designs may be seen in English works on estate decoration.

Another objection to wood in gate posts is that vines cannot be permitted to run upon them on account of the decay endangered. A gate post with any one of several vines allowed to run wild upon it is a mellowing feature, and is the initial impression which a stranger receives. If first impressions count, the entrance to a country place is very important.

The errors to be avoided in entrances are mostly connected with making them too dignified for what lies within the gates. Various instances come to our thought, of pretentious entrances leading to flimsy dwellings. The character of the dwelling should determine the character of the gateway. The facetious connection of a Queen Anne front with a Mary Ann back is repeated in a more emphatic way by a noble gate and a mean house. In most cases it would be better to emphasize the house and omit the gate entirely. If there is no one within whom you seek to prevent from going out, and no one without whom you wish to keep from coming in, why a gate?

It is more than doubtful whether gate posts, erected merely for esthetic

LITCHFIELD BROOK   POMPERAUG BANKS

A CONNOISSEUR   A SHELTON BROOK

reasons, are in the best taste. That which has no possible use is, by that very definition, unbeautiful. If, however, the gate is desired and really leads to something, some connection in the motive of architecture may be happily carried across from the dwelling to the gate. Both may be built of the same sort of material with a common line of design.

We have a choice offered us between the road and the byway on page 95. The opening to the left is, of course, one of those ancient marks where a highway was laid out by the settlers and, in process of time, was found to be unnecessary. Nevertheless the turfy path invites our willing feet to wander past the evergreens, and to find the hepatica and the shad blow of the earliest spring. It is still true, of course, that the multitude will follow the beaten highway and leave to the quiet mind a forest sanctuary no more crowded than a cathedral. Of course, the example before us shows an excellent beginning for a country place. One is irresistibly beckoned to establish a ribbon road over this disused highway, and to erect at the left on the slope above, among the tall scattering cedars, a dwelling from the native ledges, that may stand for centuries. There will always be an abundance of such opportunities, for the average man is still extremely gregarious.

Indeed, the ideal manner of selecting a country site is to watch for some such opening as this where noble trees stand, thus providing a dignified landmark for one's private road. The other method of selecting a site is to ask, who will be my neighbors? If this method is followed, one is pretty certain to get into a poor location. It is better to make one's neighborhood, than to edge in by a narrow foothold, on a neighborhood already formed. Connecticut is not so large that any part of it can be inaccessible, provided only a fair highway extends to within a reasonable distance of the position chosen for a dwelling.

The charming buttonwood shown on page 96, at the right, leads us to wonder why these noble trees have no larger place in our literature. The oak and the elm have rooted themselves deeply in English letters. Perhaps the reason is that the buttonwood is not so widely disseminated. The endlessly fantastic shapes of its branches, its huge decorative leaves, the exquisite coloring of its bark and the massive, round, smooth trunk are features of so much importance that, taken together, they lead us to the conclusion that it is a more decorative and more impressive tree, even than an elm. It is, also, generally more lofty than an oak. We await the poet of the buttonwood, and we suggest that he may find his inspiration in California where the backgrounds are perhaps more impressive. If, however, he wishes to combine his descriptions of the tree with domestic scenes, and steady-going brooks, old Connecticut has many a stimulating suggestion for his muse. It is pleasing to see young groves of buttonwood starting on some Connecticut banks, as also through New Jersey and Pennsylvania. We know no bole that suggests power, like the trunk of a buttonwood, finished almost as in a gigantic lathe. A pair of such trees flanking a cottage gives a suggestion of stability and dignity very happily combined with beauty.

The confluence of waters has an endless charm for us from the time when, scarcely removed from babyhood, we changed tiny rivulets with our toes, to the hour when on a headland we looked on the glories of Merrymeeting Bay in Maine. The wedding of two streams appealed also to the Indian whose intrinsically poetic nature induced him to give names appropriate to such conjunctions. The artistic canon is that there should not be two centers of interest in a picture, and perhaps in " Waters Meet," on page 99, there is only one main center. Yet the thought is, in the title and in the mind, of twin streams.

Very many laws of beauty have been laid down but, happily, we enjoy before we analyse. An enhanced enjoyment, however, comes to us through a study of the elements that make up beauty. Even when we arrive at no definite conclusion, the subject occupies us agreeably. Possibly the first principle of beauty consists in form or color capable of pleasing. Thus a formidable crag covered with massive black green, and the terror of a storm cloud above it, and wild water beneath it, may entrance a masculine

[*Continued on page* 129]

AN EMBOWERED COTTAGE — MYSTIC

OLD CONNECTICUT — SOUTHBURY

A DRAPED ROAD—LITCHFIELD COUNTY

FILLING THE PITCHER—LITCHFIELD COUNTY

WHITHER?

By Mildred Hobbs

Wind on, little country road!
We care not whither you lead,
For the air is sweet in the hollows,
And the wind is brisk on the hills!
Wind on, little ribbon of gold,
With your fringe of flowering weed
Where many a wild rose nestles
And many a wild bird trills!

Lure on with a beckoning hand!
We care not whither nor why —
To the soft gray heights of the mountain,
Or the dim retreats of the vale!
Wind on through the arching elms,
That circle the hills and sky
And the dreamy drift of the cloudlets.
Wind on, little vagabond trail!

For you are the road of Life,
And ours are the dusty feet,
And it's over the hills and hollows —
We know not whither nor why.
Sometimes you are rough, little road;
But there's ever a blossom sweet,
Or a fleeting glimpse of the highlands,
Or the song of a bird in the sky!

THE HOME ROAD

Written for the picture by MILDRED HOBBS

This morning when the bluebird sang
Above the well where blossoms hang,
As I was strolling by,
A road-mate flitted at my side,
Who proved a friendly little guide —
A Gypsy butterfly!
And I thought nothing could compare
With morning's lilac-scented air,
And trees and meadows gleaming fair
Beneath a sunny sky.

With bees amid the blossoms gay
I dreamed and wandered through the day
Till all was strange and white.
The little road, so still, so sweet,
With young, fresh grasses at my feet,
Was touched with mystic light.
I heard the bluebird's evening call,
And sleepy squirrels in the wall —
Oh, it is loveliest of all
Between the day and night!

For then the elms and hanging nest,
Against the dim gold of the west,
Stand lacy-leafed and tall.
Some lift their arms in evening prayer,
And others, with a sheltering care,
Above the homestead fall.
I roam by day with butterflies,
But in the twilight of the skies
The home road to my paradise
I love the best of all!

FACING THE LIGHT—NEAR MYSTIC

HADDAM ELMS

AN OAK SHORE—STONINGTON

UNLOADING THE STACK—NYACK

LAKE–SIDE

By Mildred Hobbs

By the quiet lake-side
Rhythmic ripples blend
With whispered rustlings of the leaves
Where spreading branches bend.

Sailing placid waters,
Shadow-clouds drift by,
And darting zig-zag in their wake,
A bright-winged dragon-fly.

Curving tips of grasses
Touch their sandy floor,
As straying wavelets curl and lap
The reeds about the shore.

Jewelled floating lilies
Water nymphs unfold,
To scatter sweetness in the air,
From treasure-hearts of gold.

Through the sparkling shallows
Shining minnows glide,
And far off shore the leaping trout
Leave blue rings circling wide.

Murmur of the ripples —
Swish of fern and brake —
The splashing feet of a slender deer!
How softly sings the lake!

THE MEADOW STREAM

By Mildred Hobbs

Sleeping through the warm noon's glory of the meadows,
Cool upon its moss bed lies the silent stream,
Under slumbering-robes of blue, through the haze reflecting,
Peacefully content with the day's long dream.

Dreaming of the hours when its wild, rushing music
Mingled with the rapture of the song-flooded breeze, —
Tumbled notes of bobolinks, twitter of the swallows,
Melodies of meadow-larks, high in the trees!

Dreaming of the iris with its broad, flagged petals;
Yellow-painted-cups, and their flaming, scarlet leaves;
Tender blue-eyed grass, shining buttercups and daisies;
And the colors myriad that spring interweaves!

Sleeps the cool water, through the beauty of the summer,
Turquoise and gold in the garments of the morn!
Silver cobwebs drape from the fringes of the gentian:
Fern-tips the iridescent dew-drops adorn!

Slumbering it lies there between its gay borders!
Golden rod and trumpet weed cluster on the banks;
Wild mint, dragon-heads, asters blue and purple,
Fire-weed and rose mallow crowd in gorgeous ranks!

While the idle butterflies float above the lilies,
And the trees hover with a gentle, low croon —
Dream, meadow-stream, of your springtime's rippling laughter!
Dream long dreams through the silent summer noon.

WOODBURY WATERS

NORWICHTOWN

EAST WINDSOR WATERS

THE SUNLIT POOL—EAST WINDSOR

soul, and even a feminine mind may admire, while shuddering. Thus beauty need not always consist in soft melting lines or colors, but sometimes in the vaster, more mysterious and mighty shapes that suggest infinity, and lead the thought by leaps over mountain tops and even into the far flung grandeurs of the upper air where we are carried, as in Elijah's chariot. It is not always the same mind that can enjoy equally the snowy Sierras and the field of daisies in a hollow beneath them. While the love of beauty is present in every mind, it is a dominating factor in some minds. Certainly not to admire the glories of an unrolled universe, from a snow flake to a star, is to lose most of the best out of life. How far the love of beauty may be cultivated is doubtful. It seems to be a faculty born, not made. It is nevertheless a mystery, that in certain eras very much is made of the charms of landscapes, while in others such charms are practically ignored. It is probable that the trend of human thought and attention are caused by certain leading minds, who establish a passion which shows itself in literature and society.

If we have the faculty of being pleased with the awesome and sombre and majestic, as well as with the exquisite details of a flower, we broaden our joy in living, and escape a mechanical existence. There is seldom a time in our waking hours when, if we are out of doors, nature fails to call us with one allurement or another. The very contrast between the snow-white stillness of a bitter winter day, and the teeming growths of beauty in June greatly enhances the enjoyment of each extreme. Those who dwell in a region of lofty mountains, get both these extremes in the same season. We must wait some months. In the rounded year, the stimulus of these various appeals doubtless enlarges our faculties, not only as concerns beauty but in a general way.

A Canaan Pasture (page 100) suggests a subject for Maxfield Parrish. What magnificent reds he would place on the great oaks above the stream!

In a Field Lane (page 100) on the road from Willimantic to Norwich there must be the invisible ghost of a horse. The author has a witness

[*Continued on page* 133]

THE ACORN TREE

By Mildred Hobbs

Beside the road,
The wandering breezes long ago bestowed
Upon the ground an acorn-cup, and sowed
It deep.
Asleep
It lay until an hour
When richly nurtured soil, with sun and shower,
Filled it with power
To push above the earth until it spread
A shelter overhead —
A king of trees
Who tosses to the breeze
His acorns and his shapely russet leaves,
The which a distant spot receives.
What majesty one acorn life achieves!

Beside the road,
Kind words of cheer and comfort were bestowed
Upon a heart, and through its warm depths sowed
Their seed.
The need
And hunger of the hour,
The richness of a soul, with sun and shower,
Gave them the power
To burst the darkened bondage of the night
And fill the heart with light
Which radiates
Its beauty, and creates
A strength and sturdiness and shelter there.
Kind words, like acorns, live and bear,
Beside the road, life's beauty and life's prayer.

CONNECTICUT OAK MAJESTY—HADDAM

THE HEART OF NEW ENGLAND

ON THE FARMINGTON RIVER

to maintain with him that, when this picture was made, a horse was reaching his neck over the wall. It must have been one of Conan Doyle's spirit steeds. Certainly the witches have carried it off. We have known instances where objects appeared on photographic plates which were not supposed to be there, but this is the first on record where an object that appeared to the eye was missing in the picture. However, no one cares to look at a horse or to ride one these days. It may be that sometime his vogue may return, for he is the most beautiful of all animals, possibly the most intelligent, and certainly the one mightier than any or all others in giving a cast to history, and even in shaping its trend, through the age of chivalry.

A field road like the one shown in this picture will lead the way to all sorts of joys, if only we allow the imagination to build and to inhabit its structures.

This leads us to wonder how far culture features constitute the charm of a landscape. To certain minds, such features are the be all and the end all. It depends upon how closely we associate man with nature. Certainly a lane with a cart path is more pleasing to the average person than one which shows no trace of man's foot. The hands that formed the bar way are no longer active, and those that planted the blooming trees have also finished such labors. The Chinese mind has developed to the highest degree the sense of the continuity of generations. To a Chinaman there is just as much interest in an old wall that was built by his father as there would be if he himself had erected it. Further, the more remote that father was, the more reverence does his son pay to his ancestor's work. This characteristic is not so apparent in the American mind. Yet the charm of age, and the sense that the setting of the beautiful scene before us was made by our fathers, is an element in our pleasure as we view the spot. It would probably be impossible to assign their due weight to the different elements of joy that possess us as we walk down the old lane. One of the greatest of all mysteries is the gathering up of an infinite number of appeals made to the fathers and reincarnate in us. Probably the sense of smell, which is usually associated with objects that are pleasant to look upon, is the consequence of a long evolution. Thus a dog may follow the scent of an animal, and would not notice an apple blossom. The use of perfumes, recognized from the most ancient period as an allurement or an antidote, perhaps arose through the sense of beauty.

On the Quinnebaug (page 103) is a back water reach of that pleasing stream, as seen near Jewett City. It can be found only at high water, and with spring foliage. A variant of this picture, called " Peace," is fully as beautiful.

The old recessed porches, such as were used a good deal from 1830 to 1850, like the example shown on page 104, are always rather appealing. Sometimes they were formed as arched recesses in which the front door appeared as here, but where the recess was very much smaller than here in proportion to the porch. This recess answers as a vestibule, quite effectively obviating the necessity of a second door, and protecting the doorway better than a quaint door head, and better than the more elaborate porches of the period of 1800. We suppose it is rather heretical to like work of this period, but we confess a fondness for it. At least the pillar seems to be done here in fairly classical design, and the porches are approached by a solid set of stone steps. The abomination of wooden steps anywhere about a house is much to be deplored, as they decay in a very few years, and always advertise the house as a makeshift, temporary affair.

The northwestern corner of Connecticut is very high and yet not dry. The lakes are so numerous that one district is even named Lakeville and has become a more or less well known resort. Norfolk, also, which has great local pride and much reason for it, is in this same neighborhood. We should say that Norfolk had done as much in the way of local improvement to beautify the town as any like center of the size. Approached either from Winsted or from the Berkshires it makes a good impression. Its fair homesteads and comfortable hotels shelter many who enjoy a somewhat quiet neighborhood of high moral tone.

The neighboring towns of Sharon and Salisbury have much of the

A BLOSSOM LANE—NEW HAVEN COUNTY

THE AUTUMN ROAD—LITCHFIELD COUNTY

HARTFORD BLOSSOMS

same character and attraction. Situated, as this corner of the state is, so near to New York, its merits have been appreciated by many who come from beyond New England. The district suffers at present from the lack of a good through route to the south directly through Sharon and Kent to New Milford. If such an approach is ever improved, it will afford one of the beautiful drives of Connecticut. The region is somewhat more accessible from the south than the Berkshires, and has an attraction all its own.

Kent and New Milford teem with many fine outlooks. The contours of the byways and the streams charm away many a summer day of the explorer. One is amused to find that railways are so little considered these days, but we should still remember that these regions are accessible by that means of conveyance.

Winsted, in Winchester, affords a pretty good center of investigation. We may get out from it into the hills of Barkhamstead, Hartland and Colebrook, which are among the old fashioned towns of Connecticut, although in the hills. Our limits prevent illustrations of every town, but we can assure the reader that he will find on the upper stretches of the Farmington River, and on the east branch of the same stream, many fine mirrors of fair hills. Indeed, the Farmington River, throughout its course, is one of the most pictorial streams in existence. Very recently an important project has been set on foot to form reservoirs of this stream, north of the Connecticut line, so that it may be useful as well as ornamental. It is delightful to find odd corners and back townships being brought into the arena of the great world. Water power, as well as the new means of locomotion, assist in binding together every part of our states into coördinate units. Indeed, it is a question whether those hill towns, which were despised in generations since and largely forsaken, will not be found to be more important in an economic aspect, as well as in an aesthetic sense, than the centers of population.

The immense vogue of Sheffield plate, at the end of the eighteenth and the beginning of the nineteenth centuries, seems to be returning to some degree. A little while back, old pewter was not much regarded whereas, at the present time, it is eagerly sought, especially the American specimens. The proud possessors of a fine tea urn with, perhaps, a coin silver band just below the lid, and of good old trays and candle sticks, are now very much respected by their friends.

On page 108 the daughter of the house seems engaged in polishing the family pewter. Indeed, Connecticut is the place of all others where pewter and Sheffield plate should be revived, because at Bridgeport, Waterbury, Derby and such centers an unbroken tradition of its manufacture has continued. The Brittania ware which succeeded pewter had its home here in Connecticut, and the making of sterling silver was also a considerable industry. Many an old home is decorated with grandmother's relics, or even mother's relics, of some of the fine old examples of Connecticut craftsmanship. The room shown is the dining room of the famous Webb House at Wethersfield.

Hartford has enough to hold the seeker after beauty. With roads radiating in every direction, all of them with quaint architectural monuments, and nearly all of them bordered by fine trees and crossing placid streams, it occupies a strategic position. This is a fact which needs not be told to any resident of Hartford. There is more than one particular in which it is the center of the American past. Its magnificent bridge, which for a long time was regarded as the noblest monument of its sort, the people of Springfield now claim to have surpassed. We cannot admit the claim if beauty alone is considered. We also feel that when we take into account the great causeway approaching the bridge on the east, the Connecticut structure must ever remain a massive and historic erection to gain respect from our posterity.

The vagaries of the Connecticut in flood provide the seeker after beauty with many outlines which he does not see at the usual stage of the water. It is not every stream that may be shown at different periods, quite different in its shore outlines and in all cases lovely. The Connecticut in its overflow does little damage, as its waters move with no great and

MERIDEN-STONINGTON ROAD

OVERBROOK — SOUTHBURY

SOMERS WATERS

JONATHAN EDWARDS DOOR—YALE

terrifying speed, and its rise is discounted by those who understand its habits. It is the Nile of Connecticut. The Farmington river, which finds its devious way through Simsbury and Windsor at last reaches the Connecticut. The great town of Windsor, from which South Windsor, East Windsor, Windsor Locks and, for ought we know, other towns have been carved out, is still of generous proportions, and full of fascination for the seeker after the old and the beautiful. On both sides of the Connecticut the original town of Windsor is filling up with suburban residences edging in here and there among the old houses, and affording a retreat with pleasing surroundings for those whose daily labors are in Hartford. The rich, red soil, the gently rolling contours of the landscape, the magnificent elms, the substantial farm houses, the picturesque bridges, altogether constitute a setting worthy of the people who dwell here. These landscapes are almost too regular for grandeur, but they convey a sense of native wealth such as comes to one in the prairies of the west. The like remark applies to Enfield which is a continuation of the same fair country. Enfield is becoming citified rapidly, through the carving out of Thompsonville from its side, but there are still many fair farms within its bounds. East and South Windsor spread a great and level plain before us, and are the home of the industry so dear to the smoker. They bear every evidence of a wealthy countryside, and their prosperity has stimulated the careful preservation of many of the fine, early farm houses.

There are so many beautiful homes in and about Hartford, and there is such an ingenious spirit in the people of Connecticut that we have some-times wondered whether it is not in this state that a new architecture may arise. The recent rapid development of Bridgeport and Waterbury has stimulated the erection of beautiful homes, and has enabled many architects to carry out their ideas, if not just as they desired, nevertheless with more freedom than formerly. On Prospect Avenue in Hartford, and in many other quarters in only slightly less degree, are to be found beautiful examples of homes built to last, of the most substantial materials,

[Continued on page 145]

NEW LIFE

By Mildred Hobbs

Earth wakens from her dream of death,
For in her ancient bosom hide
The rose tints of a new-born May,
And Earth is glorified!

She weaves a gorgeous blossom-cloak
For all the old and ragged trees,
And bids the leaflets on the elms
To dance upon the breeze.

She covers up her marks of age
With mossy banks and rivulets,
And young lambs gambol in her fields
Among the violets.

Are not the mysteries of May
But lovely symbols of the birth
Of One who spread the light of life
Upon a dying earth?

The Christ-child was a tender bud,
Unfolding in the light of dawn,
And bursting into perfect bloom
For all to gaze upon.

And Love broke through the crust of souls
And gave to earth a living stream
Where we, the flock, may quench our thirst
With happiness supreme.

A WAYSIDE POOL—NEW HAVEN COUNTY

NEW LIFE

LILY PAD POOL — TORRINGTON

LILAC GABLES — WITHERSFIELD

and following lines of much grace. Perhaps it is here, after Philadelphia and Boston, that we find most that is meritorious in these respects. Certainly if the size of the cities is considered, in Connecticut they seem to have a finer residence development than other parts of New England. The teeming genius of the valley of the Connecticut has set its accurate and tasteful minds at work, and has produced a very great deal of the highest merit, not so much from its magnificence, as from its excellent adaptability to need, and from its thorough good taste.

CONNECTICUT ABOUT MIDDLETOWN

THERE is no point in Connecticut better than Middletown for investigating the delightful districts of the state. A road from Middletown to East Hampton, recently completed, takes us through right and left and up and down twists, with most pleasing outlooks here and there. At East Hampton, we come upon a large body of water, Pocotopaug Lake, around which there is a road. The main highway extends to Marlboro where it connects with other fine new roads, although that part of the state is thinly populated. East Hampton adjoins the town of Chatham. It is curious in Connecticut how the local village name supplants, for travelers at least, the name of the town so that one often passes through a township not only without knowing its bounds, but even its name. Of course this is especially true in the hill country. We may now travel through most of the remote districts of Connecticut, sometimes for miles without passing a dwelling, over cement roads. In a short time the very strong trend toward road betterment in this state will reveal to the traveler many delights which have been closed to him. This condition arises out of the ancient scheme of representation in the legislature, whereby the country towns overwhelmingly outvote the cities, very much as in the former pocket borough system in England. This curious relic of an ancient past has, of course, been fought by the cities, but in vain. It is one of the oldest situations imaginable for a new country like ours. Practically the country towns can do anything they wish with the state monies. It is to their credit that they do not take still greater advantage of the cities. Just now, in the case before us, if the country representatives get together on any proposal for road building, they can carry their point, and can apportion the cost according to their liking. Of course the general public benefits, and even where a township in the remote districts pays anything on a road, it probably pays more than its proportion according to wealth.

One curious result is that lines of 'buses have been established on various roads so that one may pass, for instance, from New London to Hartford, more readily by the 'bus than by the train and over an interesting country. It is a modified revival of the English coaching system. No longer do people say that these new roads are very nice for those who have motors. The 'bus is a popular and facile method of getting about, and available for everybody. In a few minutes, starting from a great center, one may be on the backbone of the state, enjoying the waste places and far-flung views. We notice here and there a tendency to secure windy heights, in such regions, for summer homes. Such sites would be fearfully bleak in the winter, but exposed as they are on every side, often without shade, they certainly get every capful of wind that blows in summer.

It will be an interesting thing to watch the consequences of these new roads in their effect on the distribution of population.

Opposite Middletown is Portland whose name is associated with the former popular stone. This section of Connecticut, and thence west through Meriden, shows many outcroppings of a beautiful reddish-brown sandstone. It would perhaps be a heresy to state that this stone tends to scale after long exposure to the weather. It is said that on this account a great estate in New York City banned the use of the stone in its building operations. At any rate for one reason or another it fell out of fashion, and Portland has suffered as a consequence. Should the wheel of fashion shift its erratic direction, there would be possible an immense development for this part of the state, for the stone exists in unlimited quantities.

READING IN A WING CHAIR — WEBB HOUSE

HOSPITALITY HALL — WETHERSFIELD

THE YORKTOWN PARLOR, WEBB HOUSE—WETHERSFIELD

UP THE COW LANE—LITCHFIELD COUNTY

NEW ENGLAND WALLS

By Mildred Hobbs

(Written for the Picture " Up the Cow Lane.")

Old stone walls,
New England's charm,
Guard her treasure-lands
From harm,
And along
Her winding lane,
Orchards' beauty spots
Enchain.
Slender, curving,
Ribbon-shaped!
Ragged, straggling,
Blossom-draped!
Here and there, tumbled places
Where the petal-woven laces
Of a vine
Intertwine!
From the walls
Spring's happy birds
Sing to gentle
Grazing herds.
Squirrels race
Along the rocks —
Playful guardians
Of flocks.
Old stone walls
Of ages past,
Strong and sturdy,
Firm and fast —
Watchers of
The years' events —
Rugged, gray-stoned
Monuments!

We see no reason why it might not be used at least as a backing wall. It is something to make the traveler, who has associated this stone with aristocratic residences, gaze with astonishment at the foundation walls, even in barns, of this beautiful material, and in the stone walls by the roadside he sees it also. Its disintegration, entering as a large constituent into the soil, gives a warmth to the color of the ploughed fields.

Portland is possessed, in the Gildersleeve end of the town, of a stately street with four rows of magnificent trees which we show. In fact there seems to have been a breadth of spirit in the laying out of many of the early Connecticut towns, which showed itself in the spacious main streets. The main street of Hartford is, of course, the most well known instance. That of Middletown seemed too broad when the place was only a village, but is now most convenient and is fast becoming stately. Portland, Windsor, Canaan, and various other small cities and mere townships have similar streets, such as one seldom sees in Massachusetts. It is quite probable that Hooker and his companions wearied of the narrow crooked streets of Boston, and determined to avoid anything of the sort in Connecticut. It is curious, however, though intensely human, to perceive that the settlers never thought of the possibility of great cities arising out of their townships. Therefore, aside from one great thoroughfare or at most two, the second intersecting the first, the streets incline to be narrow, though they are for the most part straight, getting their lines from the original layout. Thus Asylum Street, in Hartford, is not much better than an alley in width, and the same may be said for various secondary streets in many other cities which have now become important. Where the town ceased to grow at the point where the originators intended, that is to say when it became a small center for the adjacent farming district, and when attention was given to the planting of trees, we now often have the benefit of magnificent quadruple or triple rows of shade trees, in quiet old towns, which are highly appreciated by the present generation as restful resorts. It is lamentable that carelessness here and there has permitted gas leaks to kill many of the trees.

DOUGHNUT DAY — WEBB HOUSE

LATEST FASHIONS — WEBB HOUSE

A MIDDLEBURY ROADSIDE

AN OLD MYSTIC BACK WATER

On the line of the Portland-East Hampton road, a very notable private estate has been donated to the state as a park, although there is no statement at the entrance that the grounds are public. In fact, here and in many other places, notably about the falls of Kent, one has to work one's way along, inquiring at farm houses, to learn how to reach these various public grounds. Probably the state commissioners in charge know the bounds of these state domains, but certainly nobody else does. Perhaps it is the question of appropriations, but certainly the traveler would be thankful even for a scrawl on a shingle. If one diverges at Cobalt, a village on the Portland-Chatham line, to the southward, one starts on the projected east shore road to follow down the Connecticut through the highlands to Lyme. At present this region is still unvisited, except for a little distance below Middle Haddam, where the good road ceases. We have never noticed a flagrant error in the Geological Survey Maps except in the case of this quaint village, which is there spelled Maddam! The village has more kinds of interest than any other of its size with which we are acquainted. On the steep slopes leading down to the river, with a crooked approach to the little dock, with the curious old dwellings, and public library, with here and there a noble colonial house, with a multitude of splendid elms, with interspersed blossoming apple trees, this home of the steady-going Connecticuter is one of the most fascinating villages imaginable. Indeed the various members of the Haddam family consisting of Middle Haddam, Haddam Neck, East Haddam, Hadlyme, Tylerville, Shailorville, and the various other Haddams are an interesting lot well worth anyone's acquaintance. We should say that if we were restricted to one town in Connecticut to stand for quaintness, beauty and variety we should name Haddam. Its name is quite redolent of the sweet past. It combines in a delightful way the little cottage and the fine mansion, both inhabited by people of finely marked character and with a setting of river and mountain such that the combination of people and place is remarkable. And yet this highland district is very readily accessible. The railroad, the navigable Connecticut, the fine west side highway, and the bridges at Portland and East Haddam and the ferry at Hadlyme, bring the section within a few minutes of Middletown, and a few minutes more to Hartford or, southerly, to the mouth of the river. In short the district is no bad epitome of early Connecticut.

Near Moodus is a wild region of seven lakes large enough to lay down on the map, besides numerous smaller unnamed gem-like ponds. Here is the locally named Devil's Hop Yard, though we find no such name on a map. It is a remote neighborhood of fantastic cliffs, deep vales, and wild scenery destined to be better known. At present perhaps the best access is from Lyme through Hamburg. If there were here and there a guide post to such regions, the investment would pay heavy dividends.

Essex is counted by its old friends among the most fascinating Connecticut villages. The river in this vicinity spreads into bays, lagoons and long fingers. It is a natural watering place and reminds one somewhat of the fen country of England. Deep River claims for itself the crown among New England villages, and while that aspiration may be pretentious it has something to justify it, and it is especially pleasing to find an appreciation by the inhabitants of a district of its own charm, — a thing which is often lacking. Indeed it is somewhat startling to enter a village and be met by a large sign announcing that you are on the threshold of a queen. It is by such appreciation as this that a village more and more seeks to make good its claim. Though a counsel of perfection may be unattainable, as in human character, so in a town the effort to grade it and strengthen it, and lend it dignity and give it purity, is akin to the moral side. Above Deep River in Chester is another quaint neighborhood. The river here, a view of which we show, is broken in its shallows by grasses and tongues of varied vegetation. Altogether in this neighborhood we are pulled about by sweet allurements from one village to another. It is not surprising that many persons find life very enriching and satisfying here.

The fact that the main body of motor travel goes from Hartford through Meriden to New Haven, and so on to New York, leaves the

A LEAN-TO AMONG BLOSSOMS—NEW HAVEN COUNTY

THE HISTORY OF THE REVOLUTION—WEBB HOUSE

THE GLEN BROOK—REDDING

THE FIRST LEAVES—SOUTH SHORE

road from Hartford to Saybrook, where these charming villages lie, somewhat free from the crowd.

Let no one suppose it is feasible to garner the best of a countryside from a rapid tour through it. One requires, to get the true flavor, to remain a little in each village and to know, at least slightly, some of its people. We Americans are accused of being superficial. It will not advantage us to retort that those who make the accusation are equally shallow, even if their shallow spots and ours do not coincide. The motor car will tend further to spread our casual glance over great parts of America, if we love the superficial. At the same time, the motor car enables us to penetrate little villages and odd corners, and thus those that care to study intimately a little neighborhood, may be the better able to do so.

For instance the library at Middle Haddam (p. 85) with its wide end overhang is, although somewhat restored, a characteristic early feature that will not be seen on the broad highway. In the same village on a side street, on a sharp slope, is the gable of a house having a Palladian window, a very rare and dignified feature for a gable. As seen over the lilacs, it has an individuality and charm which helps to classify the neighborhood.

The tree variously called buttonwood, button-ball and sycamore, favors the water side, and usually leans over the stream, as on page 115.

The very interesting and decorative corner cupboards like that on page 116, are characteristic of Connecticut, especially if in their lower doors they have a St. Andrew's cross panel. We went back the other day to see again the old dwelling where this cupboard was, but found only a cellar hole. It was a sharp and important lesson as to the necessity of recording the architectural and landscape features of a neighborhood. The very road where this dwelling was found, had been lifted and changed, and the river made into a lake. We want to know the atmosphere of the life of our ancestors. Some day we may see fit to try to reproduce it.

The Virginia rail fence, otherwise sometimes called a snake fence, which appears on the bottom of page 119, is a picturesque feature of parts of Connecticut. It is seen also on page 135 in a very charming location under the apple and maple boughs. Where the rails intersect, the woodbine, or some other growth, ties together the corners. Where rails were plenty, it was the simplest of all fences, being composed solely of rails which could be laid up with great rapidity, so that one man might build in a day a long section. We remember also that the old price in the country for laying a stone wall, was a dollar a rod. We do not doubt that the owners of some estates have paid a hundred times as much, and then spoiled the quaintness of the effect by laying their stones in mortar.

Along the shore of Long Island Sound the farmer's commodities used to be loaded and unloaded, as we are reminded by the picture " Unloading the Stack " on page 124. As the waterways were the roads of the settlers, the Sound became their greatest boulevard. Here is a rarely seen thing, a barge load of loose hay which must indeed have been very picturesque as it floated along, as if a hay stack had gone to sea. In fact, if one's mind were a little dull, one might well rub one's eyes at such a sight.

The Sound, while beautiful to look upon, is not generally favorable for pictorial work of the kind found in this book. The scenes are too broad and flat. They are more favorable for oil paintings, as the colony of artists at Miss Griswold's in Lyme has demonstrated. All the country round about Lyme has served as a setting for many a picture during a period of long years. Miss Griswold's broad roof has sheltered a large number of artists, who have left her souvenirs in the form of painted panels throughout the old dwelling, a rare and distinguished feature.

The region around Meriden contains many lakes which serve for power or for city reservoirs, and always for decoration. The red cliffs coming down by steps, so fine a feature of central Connecticut, are often mirrored in the streams and the pools of the region. The apple orchards beneath these cliffs combine their white with the warm tinted cliffs towering above them. This is a region of wide plains in spite of its craggy masses. Southington lies broad and fair beneath its mountain. This same moun-

HARKNESS QUADRANGLE—NEW HAVEN

SINGING STONES — GREENWICH

THE REDDING GLEN

tain was once an almost insuperable barrier to acquaintance between the valleys which it divided, but is now a mountain of delight, as we quickly and easily reach its crest, and look abroad on the teeming valleys at either side. It is a rare town in Connecticut, even if the ground is nearly level, that lacks its rippling or silent stream. Whether rushing from the hills and complaining ever at the obstructing rocks, or moving silently, mirrorlike, over the meadows, the waters of Connecticut are always intriguing. In so many instances they have done their work at the various industrial plants, past which they have now flowed, that they can afford a leisurely course. They have expended their strength, and now they show their beauty. We are ever inclined to bare our heads reverently by the side of the streams. Their plenty is so lacking in most regions of the earth, that the worship of waters amongst the ancients, in arid zones, was not only natural but almost inevitable. When one thinks of the meagre streams, quickly lost in the sand, of Syria, of Egypt, of Australia, one cannot be grateful enough for the superabundance of waters so emphatically called to our attention by every drive in New England. As water means a bridge, it has given men an opportunity to throw chords of beauty, majestically large or quaintly small, over this flowing mystery that is ever coming from the sea to cloud, to mountain, to meadow and to sea again.

Bridges stand for peace, and the unity of human thought. A bridge as a far finer monument than a pillar. We are amused at reading how the people of Ipswich, and doubtless of various Connecticut towns, looked askance at the first stone arch thrown across a stream in their neighborhood. In one Connecticut town it was freely predicted that, when the false work was taken out, the bridge would fall. Even at this time of supposed diffusion of knowledge, the principle of the arch is rarely understood. The arch always imparts a charm to a landscape. The author was guilty, while abroad, of picturing more than three hundred bridges. A bridge itself is a continual visible triumph, leaping as it does across the unstable and often fearsome floods. The crested bridges of Spain are here and there being reproduced in somewhat less emphatic form in our country. Great new bridges at Devon and numerous other places in Connecticut are giving an air of stability and finish.

It was scarcely less than a decade ago that the author toured the Pacific coast by motor, and in one day passed through seventy fords. Some of them were so deep and broad that the companion of his travels had her heart in her mouth. All that is now changed. It is almost impossible for us to imagine the experience of a traveler, in a new country, who at every stream must ford, or swim, or resort to a ferry, which last mode of conveyance was available only at the more important points. Probably no one feature of civilization means so much as a bridge. It is at once architectural, commercial, social, historical. The sense that so many feet have traveled over it, that it has withstood the storms, that it has bound communities together, that it has beautified its valley, is borne in upon us daily. Rome after two thousand years is remembered by her bridges more than any other feature of her life. Away up in Wales and the north of England, in remote passes of the Balkans, and of Asia Minor, are those eternal structures which bound together the jurisprudence, the literature, the politics and the religion of the known world. We may be sure that long after our sky scrapers are dust, our best bridges will bring blessings to us from the remotest generation. The adaptation of architecture to use rather than to what is merely monumental, reaches its climax in a bridge, which in its winding approaches, and in the various devices to which its builder must resort to meet the individual character of the stream below, offers always an opportunity for that ever charming combination of use and beauty.

The author is deeply indebted to bridges because, standing upon them, he has obtained hundreds of his pictures.

A bridge in the country lies in the memory of almost every boy who has fished or played about it. The narrow rim of earth which perhaps lay between its buttress and the stream, was his hiding place and fortress, when his castle was stormed by his companions. It is much to be feared

A PICTURE BROOK—SOUTH SHORE

ALL THE NEWS AND MORE—NEW HAVEN COUNTY

AT THE POUR-OVER—SALEM

WILDWOOD BLOSSOMS—EAST HARTFORD

also, that when this boy was looked for by those who had some task to lay upon him, he often found refuge in this hiding place. The trout, also, that dashed through, were more clearly visible by the shadow of the bridge. In later years, leaning on the rail above, he found the girl who to his mind was the village belle and, standing there between the changing water below and the changeless sky above, they plighted their troth for eternal things in a mutual world. The Bridge of Sighs is historical, but a bridge of laughter or of affection is perhaps, at least so we hope, a more usual bridge.

No one can forget that the bridge has proved the fortress and the place of defense for many a patriot from the time of Horatius to that of the Minute Men. The imagination of the average citizen may be dull, but we observe that the names of the selectmen who erect a bridge are invariably inscribed upon it in these days.

THE GROWTH OF A DWELLING

CONNECTICUT contains, perhaps, more sorts of old houses than any other part of the country, and it is in this state that we may pause to notice the growth of the idea of a dwelling, in America.

How soon men graduated from caves we do not know, nor are we greatly concerned. The main thing is that they came out, and for the most part stayed out, in spite of the recrudescence of cave men in literature. In practice there are a few scattered relics of cave dwellings among civilized men, as in France. The dwellings of the aborigines under the cliffs of the arid southwest can hardly be called cave dwellings, as they were erected, stone by stone, the cliff forming more a fortification than a part of the structure.

Americans in New England, at least, had, as their first thought, the idea of immediate protection from the severity of our winters. For this purpose they found logs the most readily available material and it is the boast of Webster, in his speech in the log cabin campaign, that his father erected a log cabin in New Hampshire. Such cabins are still common in the Appalachian and the Rocky Mountains. They are warm and durable, as wood is a nonconductor. The interstices, chinked with moss and mud, were made air tight. The cross sections of the log, overrunning at the ends, gave a picturesque effect. The chimneys were laid of mud and sticks or stone. The floors were of beaten clay, or flagstones. The windows were paper or simply clear openings to the day, protected by a solid shutter at night. The solid shutter idea has prevailed in some sections of our country down to the present day, and in this year of grace the author has seen a considerable number of new dwellings in Pennsylvania with such shutters. Their protective character is, in the thought of these modern builders, a good feature, but the main feature is probably decorative as such shutters are often made with panels. The door was of handsawed plank, usually double, the outer course being vertical and the inner course running crosswise, thus constituting a barrier of much ruggedness and strength. This was about all there was to a dwelling. Sometimes only a ladder led to the loft. If the house was of one room, as frequently occurred at first, the chimney, of course, was at the end, and sometimes the roughly broken stone constituted the whole end, the logs there being omitted.

The next step was the two room house with a chimney in the center, fireplaces on both sides and a small entry at the front door with a stair narrow and steep, with its side facing the door and its rear side against the chimney. The first windows were casements, that is to say, hinged sash either single or double, the joint running up and down, and the glass being of diamond pattern set in leads, which, be it noted, did not cross each other at regular intervals. The glass was set in diagonal rows, one row at a time, so that on the next course the cross section of the lead would perhaps not coincide exactly with the diagonal lines of the previous row. This is a nice little point that has not been noticed, at least not thought

THE JOY OF THE FOREST—HARTFORD COUNTY

SPRING LIGHTS—SOUTH WINDSOR

A SPRING NEST—EAST HARTFORD

PATH, BLOSSOM, AND CANAL—EAST HARTFORD

worth while to imitate, by all modern architects. There were also generally a couple of small cross bars of wood, with wires soldered into the
lead to stiffen the sash.

The next step in houses was the use of the half timbered English
house reproduced in America. We have not remaining any such dwellings
among us. We have a number of planked or boarded houses, inside of
which the walls are filled in between the framing timbers with rubble or
with brick. It is still a question among architects whether any of these
houses were originally built as simple half timbered dwellings, and
whether the outside coating of boards or planks was subsequently added.
At any rate, this addition was found to be advisable in the American
climate, subject to much greater extremes than that of England. These
extremes open joints between the timbers and the masonry. The great
abundance of wood suggested a veneer of it as protection to what would
otherwise have been a plain half timbered house.

The cobble work construction was finished either directly upon the
masonry on the inside, by plaster, or irregularly split lath was first applied.
Partitions were formed of matched boards with very long tongues, in the
panel style, so that the name " sheathed paneling " has been applied to
this construction, though there is no true top and bottom of the panel.

The interior doors were made precisely like the sheathed walls, and
were cleated. The paneled door came in later. Some doors are found
of a single board without a cleat.

The first floor of wood was in the form of puncheons, that is to say,
logs split in the middle and laid with the flat side uppermost. The
earliest houses had no cellars. As soon as cellars came in, pit-sawed
boards were laid on floor timbers, and at first it is probable that many
floors were single, as were the floors of the lofts. The widest boards
possible were used. They are now sometimes found two feet in width,
and anything less than sixteen inches was thought rather mean. The
first cellar was approached from a trap door and a ladder, and was
often under one room only. Shortly after, the stair to the cellar was

built under the front stair, and either opened up to the front entry or by a door by the side of the chimney. The cellar wall, in Connecticut at least, could often be laid up of stones having a natural cleavage, and requiring no other tools for its preparation except a heavy hammer. This remark applies not only to the sandstone, but to the stratified granite. The cellar walls were generally laid dry. The same sort of stone was used for door steps and paths. In the case of the stratified granite, fine glinting bits of mica in its structure gave it a beautiful surface, gleaming in the sun with a soft and delightful effect. Very slight wear rendered these stones smooth. With the coming in of the stone chimney, which was laid, especially in Connecticut, owing to the abundance of this stone in that state, as well as in Rhode Island, we have the finest characteristic feature of our early American houses. Appearing in fireplaces, as in the Hamilton Holt house at Woodstock, this stone imparts an air of wonderful stability to a home room. One feels that such a dwelling is built for the ages, and forms a fireside worth defending. The hearth-stone was really such, being as a rule in one great slab, now often found broken owing to strain, or the spilling of water upon it while it was hot.

The fireplace, at first, had its stout lug pole of wood followed later by the crane. Lug chains and huge trammels adjusted the height of the kettles to the fire. One such trammel of great size, with a saw tooth edge and a scrolled surface, has also the date 1697 cut upon it, and is in the author's collection. The interesting thing is that it has no hook at the top, but a great ring through which the lug pole must have been passed, to remain there until it charred away.

Fireplace devices were of an amazing variety, and were not as simple as has often been supposed. They extended in number to between one and two hundred in a large household. Even one double boiler has been discovered, so arranged that one kettle was hung within, another upon a crane. The well shaped holder with its rows of skewers, the roasting spit with its weighted jack, and andirons with their hooks to

THE EXUBERANCE OF MAY—MIDDLESEX COUNTY

A LITTLE OLD DAM—SALEM

FLOWER OF THE LILY

hold it, were the main factors of the fireplace, of course. But the number of pots and pans and kettles and skillets was legion. The quaintest utensils of all were big forks, spoons, skimmers and flapjack turners. The first thing the restorer of an old fireplace does today is to hasten into place a huge and lofty pair of English andirons, never or very rarely used in this country. In fact, we do not remember ever to have seen any such that were anciently here. The andirons had to be removed when the great back log was put in place on its low subordinate fire dogs. A very lofty andiron was absolutely unusable as being always in the way. The styles were almost always quite simple and twenty inches high or under.

The variety of the toasters with their spiraled sections and their quaint handles runs into the hundreds. Some of them were doubtless intended as gifts to the sweetheart or wife. The broilers, also, were in some cases very intricate, having hollowed bars draining into a hammered trough with a spout for catching the meat juice. The trivet which in general, in England, we find in brass was in the early American examples of iron, and in very many forms. A full description of a fireplace may be left for development elsewhere. Here we need only say that it was a complete armory of household utensils and a museum of ingenuities in iron. It was huge, broad, high and deep.

As soon as bricks were burned, which was done very early, square clay tile, unglazed and laid close together, was used for the hearths all over the house. In the great fire room there were generally three rows of these tiles projecting into the room, each tile being about seven and a half inches square. In some instances, however, the tile work was continued over a great part of the floor and the claim has been made that it sometimes covered the entire room. The effect was most charming.

We do not find that the lintel of the fireplace, otherwise called the chimney tree, was in the first instance of stone or iron. The largest specimens are in bog oak, hewn away to a slant on the inside below, to catch the smoke. It became very hard in the process of time. In spite of the close proximity of the great blaze we have never heard of a house catching fire from the lintel, although we have seen immense fires built in such fireplaces. In most cases there was no mantel, for the very simple reason that there was very little room for it, and nothing to attach it to except the stone, which was pretty thoroughly covered with hanging utensils.

Undoubtedly, at the very first, the fireplace and the hearth were thought of as more than half of the house. Everything else was subordinate. The size of the timbers, however, especially the corner posts and great gable girt, sometimes ran to fifteen inches square, and summer-beams are known that considerably exceed this measurement one way. The posts were hewn away on a bevel a foot or so below the point at which the girts came in, forming what is called the gun stock post. The great beams were usually chamfered, sometimes with a handsome molding and the fine chamfer stop. In fact, the beams which constituted the girt were the origin of the cornice, afterward imitated in boards and plaster in the eighteenth century, and disappearing entirely in the nineteenth century, a loss much to be lamented as, aside from the fireplace, it constitutes the main beauty of a room. The ceiling was at first left open to the floor above; then plastered between the floor joists, and a good deal later was completely lathed and plastered.

For warmth and elegance all the walls in the better houses were often sheathed. Some of the early sheathing is laid horizontally, but for the most part it was vertical.

The window frames were substantial pieces of oak or pine which projected strongly on the exterior, and were pinned together with great oak pegs.

The roofs of the very first houses were probably, for the most part, quite steep, being covered with thatch which forms a much safer roof if the pitch is strong. The material for thatch was undoubtedly marsh grass, the finer thatch of grain straws coming later.

UP THE VALE — SOUTH WINDSOR

DEEPDENE WATERS — GRISWOLDVILLE

STATELY OLD CONNECTICUT — MIDDLETOWN

RIVER BANK DRIVE — MIDDLETOWN

We have heard of very ancient tile roofs in this country. That is a special department of knowledge. After the thatch came the long shingles, and then the shorter shingles of shaved pine, which pine existed in vast quantities, and grew with a straight and easily riven grain. These shingles on a steep roof would last for a long generation, and on a side wall there are some seventeenth century houses still remaining with the original shingles.

We have mentioned the use of boards or planks on the side walls to cover masonry. It is possible that these boards finished with a bead were laid with a slight lap in some instances. A little later there was first a boarding, and then a shingling or clapboarding laid six inches to the weather with beaded clapboards of oak, followed by pine a little later yet.

There was no possible reason for the use of the oak except the English custom. Pine actually lasted longer and was infinitely easier to work. While shingles are supposed to have been used earlier than clapboards, we are not persuaded that this was the case, and it is a difficult matter to prove.

The house next following the sorts that we have been describing was the framed overhang house. This consisted of a dwelling built at one side, or one end, or both, and possibly in some instances on three sides, so that the second story jutted over the first story by about a foot and a half. Sometimes there was a square porch at the center of the side, also made with a projection. This projection seems to have varied in width according to its length. That is to say, around such a porch the length, being short, the overhang would perhaps not be over a foot.

The idea of the overhang was sometimes further carried out on the gable above the second story, but in that case it was necessary to support it by brackets. The overhang over the first story was, on the side, supported by a projection of the floor beams. A bracket might be used on the end of the same story. We doubt whether any other purpose was in the mind of the builders in America except that of following the old-world fashion, which of course was not necessary here as there was plenty of ground. Nevertheless our ancestors often built narrow streets, and huddled their dwellings just as they had in the old world, and thus secured more room upstairs by the use of the overhang.

This overhang was finished by projecting the corner posts down through it and finishing them as drops, quaintly sawed in the form of reversed finials.

The overhang house was often, if not usually, built with sharp roofs and with the two or three sharp side gables of the same pitch as the main gable.

It cannot be claimed for the overhang house that it has an air of restfulness, because it appears somewhat top-heavy. In practice its principal advantage was the protection of the lower stories from the drip of rain, and the consequent greater warmth and durability secured.

We are constantly led to wonder at the rarity of stone houses. The material which we have mentioned as so thoroughly suitable for masonry in Connecticut, may have been used in the erection of some seventeenth century houses all of stone. If, however, such is the case they have escaped our more or less cursory search. The English dwellings being often constructed of stone, and being taken as the model of the American dwelling, would seem to have been the natural thing to reproduce here. The reader, however, is invited to go up and down the Connecticut highways and byways and count the Connecticut houses of the seventeenth century in stone. The nineteenth century saw a good deal of commercial and domestic construction in this material, as around Willimantic. It is undoubtedly true that a house of wood is drier and warmer than a stone house, unless the latter is constructed by modern methods with a dead air space in the walls, such as was unknown entirely in the ancient day. One of the dearest of our friends lost his life in the great war through a recurrence of pulmonary trouble, caused by being billeted in a foreign stone dwelling, from the interior wall of which the water could be wiped off. Whether or not this consideration entered into the

SKIRTING THE ARROWANA—MIDDLETOWN

A TURBULENT CREEK—CHAPLIN

THE GLEN PASS—REDDING

SPRING SHADOWS—CROMWELL

thought of our ancestors we do not know. We do feel certain that a stone structure of a simple sort did not involve expense any greater than a wooden structure.

Building of brick was early resorted to, and the statement that the bricks of a certain dwelling were brought from England only indicates that the ships that brought them needed ballast. Brick yards were early in use here. The material was abundant and it was heavy, and there was no possible reason of bringing it across an ocean except that just stated. In fact, unless the dwellings were erected immediately on the shore of navigable waters, the transport of brick would have been impossible. The mortar used was often made of clam or oyster shells and was therefore of the best character. But well back in the seventeenth century we find stone lime being exported from Connecticut, and there are the remains of various lime kilns of very ancient origin.

By the latter part of the seventeenth century very substantial houses of ten or more rooms were not uncommon. Before the eighteenth century came, it is probable that the hewn overhang house came into vogue. There are hundreds and probably thousands yet remaining in Connecticut in this style. The post was hewn away from the bottom of the second story to the ground for about seven inches on the outside. In this sort of construction no support was necessary in the form of brackets, though brackets were sometimes used in a kind of intermediary style as in Guilford, Glastonbury, and perhaps elsewhere. The pitch of the roof decreased until, from 1780 to 1810, we find the four-chimney house built with a pitch too low to withstand the weather.

The gambrel roof appears in England at a date considerably anterior to any example found in this country. Just as Paris fashions get into the backwoods a year or two after their appearance on the boulevards, so styles in architecture and furniture in the early day of sailing ships and greater conservatism of method, were anywhere from ten years to a generation behind the English fashion. The gambrel roof so common in Connecticut, both in the cottage type and in the large two story house, was in its heyday in the middle of the seventeenth century, from which time it dated back perhaps twenty years and forward perhaps ten more. Unfortunately its vogue was brief, since its contour is pleasing. The upper roof of the gambrel has not, it is true, a sufficient pitch to bear our winters, but when we have said that, we have said the only thing against it.

The steeply pitched roof slanting on every side of the stately dwellings erected in the sixth and seventh decades of the eighteenth century, covered houses of a very high type. The woodwork of the interior was of the best. The beautiful bonnet top doorheads were the rule upon houses of this sort, as well as on the larger gambrel roofed houses.

It is not worth while to enter upon the description of the less worthy dwellings of the waning period 1780 and onward. It was a time of large and well built dwellings so far as the carpentry was concerned, but the lower roofs, the absence of cornices, the disappearance of good porches, and various other declinations of style such as the inferior mantels, incline us to direct our attention more particularly to the earlier time.

Wethersfield is somewhat rich in large square houses built around 1750. Any time after 1730 we may look for the long hall extending through the house, and the stair running to a landing, behind which there was a Palladian or at least an arched window.

The Dutch cottage of one story, with its wide-sweeping projection at the eaves, is found rarely in Connecticut, and when so found was probably built by the few Dutch settlers from New York who came into this corner of New England. The house is quite characteristic and pleasing, but we may leave it for further treatment under New York and Pennsylvania.

While it is a question of taste what sort of dwelling in wood is the most attractive, we think that the weight of modern opinion inclines to the gambrel roof. In fact, it is very seldom that we see the fine type of high pitched roof slanting to all sides, common in 1760 and with

BLOSSOM POND — MIDDLEBURY

COMMERCIAL CONNECTICUT — EAST HARTFORD

SLIDING WATERS—MIDDLESEX COUNTY

THE BUTTONWOOD TREE—MIDDLETOWN

fine dormer windows. In this connection we ought to state that the
dormer window is not common and generally not proper in the gambrel
type or those that precede it.   Our love for quaintness and simplicity
should lead, as we believe, to the rejuvenescence of the gambrel roof
in the one story variety.   Such a dwelling, with a small kitchen built
with a wing, and with the same gambrel and without dormers, affords good
windows on the gable end and six large rooms which is enough for
the average modern family.   In fact that family, if it goes on at its
present rate of diminution, will get on well with the one room house
of the first settlers.

HOW TO KNOW OLD HOUSES

ALL houses built before 1795 used hand wrought nails.   The nail
making machine, invented about that time, quickly supplanted
the wrought nail.   This is therefore a very definite means of dating,
in a negative way.

All early houses, if clapboarded, lapped the ends of the clapboards
in a long bevel.   It was a custom, also, to show less and less of the
width of the clapboard to the weather as the sill of the house was
approached.   Thus, as we look at the side of an old house, the eye,
starting with the sill and being cast upwards toward the eaves, sees the
width of the clapboards increasing.

In seventeenth century houses there is generally a very wide skirting
board above the sill, before the beginning of the clapboards.   The
barge board on the gable was sometimes put on after the clapboarding.
There is never any projection of the gable boarding, that is, no pendent
end.   The shingling is finished practically flush with the barge board.

The windows of all seventeenth houses are small.   The sash, for the
most part before 1700 and sometimes up to 1720, was leaded.   Sometimes from 1700, and generally from 1720, the sash was of wood.

Some square leaded sash has been discovered which probably dates from the seventeenth century. A wooden sash, provided with very small glass, beginning with four by six and proceeding to five by seven, seven by nine and so on, followed the leaded period. This glass is always imperfect and often iridescent. The sash is thin invariably, and broad in the muntins, in contrast to the later sash which is thick with thin muntins. No house before 1760, and probably not before 1780, had light muntins. The windows are the surest indication of age, if they remain in place. However, very few old houses retain their original sash. Many of them have the third, and some the fourth set. If, in any part of a house, an ancient sash can be found, that is sufficient to date all. The first sash known to slide, dates from 1717, and even that was leaded. Practically there are no leaded windows in place now; there is an occasional casement in an attic.

Oak clapboards indicate the seventeenth century, and are found beaded. Pine clapboards were also used at that period. Long shingles are no sure indication of age. They were used in certain districts into the eighteenth century. It was a matter of local convenience or taste. Old shingles are invariably worn thinner on their weathered portion. Any shingle which is practically of its original thickness, is surely modern.

The very earliest houses, if they had porches, had no special ornamentation about the porch. That is to say, there are probably no ornamental or bonnet top doorheads before 1730 or about that time. Previous to that there was a small vestibule with a gable, if a porch existed. But in many instances there was no porch at all. The open porch with large pillars comes in after the Revolution. The semi-elliptic glass over the front door is never early. The first instances are probably after 1780 and mostly after 1790. The side lights and sash divisions of this latest period are often done in scrolled iron work.

The half round moulding on the panels of front doors as well as in the interior of a house is the last good style, and went out in the latter part of the eighteenth century.

MERIDEN CLIFFS AND WATERS

UNDER THE HILLS—MERIDEN

GREENWICH WATERS

A BROOKFIELD DOOR

GREETED AT THE GATE

In Connecticut any house dating before 1820 had large chimneys. Before 1740 chimneys were often, if not generally, of stone. There was always a fireplace in every principal room downstairs; and we remember no instance in which a large chamber failed of having a fireplace. The larger the fireplace, broadly speaking, the older the house. The kitchen fireplace was the largest, and the chamber fireplaces were quite small, even in the earliest period.

A house to be considered old and in good style must have cornices or beams around each room, downstairs at least. The beams were open across the room, up to the eighteenth century. A plain, square meeting of the wall with the ceiling is an abomination never found in an ancient house. The cornices were not always the same about four sides of a room. The cornice being in the form of a beam, plain or ornamented, was often more prominent against the outside wall.

As to the height of ceilings, there was a considerable variation. Most seventeenth century houses were low in the ceiling, and not a few of them so low that a modern man with his hat on would scrape the summer beam. Many of the doors have openings less than six feet high. This is almost a sure indication, and a very interesting one, that physical stature is greater now than it used to be. This curious evidence is borne out by the suits of armor which are found to be too small for the average man of today. A height of six feet ten inches under a summer-beam is generous. There are some instances, however, in the latter part of the century, as in the Hazen Garrison House at Haverhill, where there was an evident effort at copying an English dwelling. In such cases the ceiling perhaps runs up a foot to a foot and a half more, even to eight feet and higher.

The plaster is generally somewhat rough. In some cases in seventeenth century houses it ran to the very floor, and a band of black was painted upon it as a baseboard. There is no absolute rule in such cases. The lath, however, of all ancient houses is made of split and irregularly spread material; never of laths cut in modern fashion.

The age of a house cannot be estimated at all by the surface of the timber. In some instances as early as 1650 we find sawed timber, and in some instances well into the nineteenth century we find hewn timber. It was a matter of convenience or taste. Where, however, the timber was hewn it was never left rough, where it was intended to show. The modern method of showing the axe cuts is thoroughly silly, as it finds no counterpart in an early house. The summer beams after being hewn were roughly smoothed with short planes, or by some other process. The same is true of the exposed girts, and the smaller floor joists and the great corner posts. It is only in the attic that the rough hewing is found.

The size of the timbers is a rough indication of the age of a house. The surest indication, however, is found in the method of framing, as shown in the complete and admirable illustrations in Mr. Isham's books. A complicated and expensive scheme of mortice and tenon was employed until the latter part of the seventeenth century. This method of framing is the finest mark of style. Of course every meeting of timbers large or small, even in dwellings through the eighteenth century, was framed. No nails were used in the construction of a frame until the balloon style of building came in with the Victorian age, or after.

Nails, however, had their place in the very earliest dwellings, and we find them freely used in floors, doors, sheathing, lathing, boarding, etc.

There is a dispute which may require some years to settle as to the earliest paneling of American houses. We know that panel work was used in furniture of the earliest period. The first chests and cupboards, made in America, were formed with true panels. Panels were also in common use in England when Connecticut was settled. It would seem somewhat daring to state that no panel work was used in construction of dwellings in the seventeenth century. Nevertheless it is very rare and, if found, it is to be looked for in diagonal panels on the facing of

A LITTLE ONE FOR THE TWINS

RIVER HAZE — MIDDLETOWN

BROOK MUSIC—NEW HAVEN COUNTY

BOYS FISHING

stairways. Ordinarily speaking, paneled rooms must be dated in the third decade of the eighteenth century or later.

The dropping of the floor below the sill of a house, so that one must step over the sill on entering, and so that a portion of the sill showed against the outside walls of a room, is a mark of the first period. We find it in the Fairbanks house at Dedham and in dwellings at Saugus, Gloucester, Wrentham and elsewhere. This section of the sill, which was left exposed, corresponded in shape and size with the girt which we may otherwise call the cornice. Instances are known of the legs of pieces of furniture, like chests, being cut shorter on the back to rest upon this injutting sill.

The hardware used upon dwellings is another approximate method of dating them. The author has shown in " Furniture of the Pilgrim Century," especially in the revision of that work, dated examples of hinges, latches and fireplace furniture. In general, it may be said that the combined strap and butterfly hinge is found on seventeenth century houses, and the wrapped joint butterfly hinge on small doors of that date. The pin butterfly hinge probably dates from about 1700, and was used a good deal in the former half of the eighteenth century. The latch is more difficult to date. The finer specimens are not generally found until the second half of the eighteenth century.

As one looks at a dwelling from the outside one always sees that a seventeenth century house sets low on the ground, with no stone underpinning visible. In fact, the difficulty is to keep these houses above ground. As a rule, the later the house the more does the underpinning show.

These remarks on early houses are offered as contributing to the complete picture of Connecticut life in its mellower and earlier aspects, and as having to do with the beauty and charm of the state.

DESCRIPTIONS OF PICTURES

THERE is a most hopeful revival of true Gothic architecture, as applied to college and school use. The wonderful buildings erected and projected at Yale University, and forming the Harkness Quad, have given an atmosphere to the city of New Haven and to some extent to the state at large. Here and there other worthy erections are observed, for ecclesiastical or scholastic use. We may feel certain that the example set at Yale will be followed in general by American institutions, and that we shall escape the somewhat mixed and not thoroughly worthy architecture, that has now been supplanted by purer and nobler styles. If we can escape the unreasoning and illogical trend of the southwest for Spanish architecture, which has no place in our climate, and does not match with our tradition, we are probably safe. This danger, however, of the Spanish styles, is imminent and must constantly be fought. It has seemed to many who are anxious to see a more beautiful America, that we should never get out of the dumps in architecture. When we remember, however, that it has required many hundreds of years for England and the continent to get their architectural atmosphere, we may take courage. Probably, within the lifetime of many now born, there will be a very great spread of the noblest designs in architecture, not only through Connecticut, but through the country as a whole. Some dominating edifice will rise in every town to give a certain solidity and dignity as an ideal to be sought. City planning is now rife. No doubt we shall make some errors. In the main, however, we believe that fifty years will revolutionize American feeling as regards public buildings, and that it will be thought a crime to erect any structure, the style of which has not been stamped with the approval of the ages. Many forget that the style of an edifice cannot be changed at will like a garment, with every spring fashion. Edifices that are worthy are built for the ages, and they require the stamp of great minds, the approval of the foremost

AN ABANDONED LANE—NEW HAVEN COUNTY

CEDAR PASTURE—PORTLAND

BREAKING A WAY—WINCHESTER

AN ANCIENT WOOD—NEWFIELDS

artists and engineers. A gaudy, or extravagant, or flimsy note in costume can be gotten rid of quickly. He, however, who wrongs this and successive generations by an ugly and tasteless structure, has deprived youth of inspiration and nobility, as expressible in architecture. As the ancient architects builded better than they knew, we have built worse than we knew. We have forgotten the normal note in architecture. We have failed to see that a flimsy structure not only endangered life, which is precious, but still further has endangered noble ideals, which are more precious. The erection of any good edifice, however small, is a challenge to rise. It is a bulwark for human character and a sign and symbol to be quoted. Edifices, when they are noble, get into literature and life. Strong and beautiful public buildings will inevitably be followed by dwellings of a better character. A substantial church in good taste will, in process of time, change the architecture of an entire village. It is time for a crusade for dignified homes. The cry for better housing of our people arises out of the sense of the dignity of human nature. The man is reflected in his home. If he lives in a den or a shack he will be a barbarian or a sloven. Poor building means poor thinking. Tawdry building means shoddiness of character. Dishonest building reflects a dishonest person. Anything that is good in form or substantial in character, which stands continually before the eyes of men, is bound to elevate their standards of life. Having said all this, we are almost ready to say that bad architecture is immoral. How can an intelligent man worship God honestly in an edifice with wooden, hollow, sanded, imitation Gothic buttresses? You can keep the worshipers in such an edifice honest only by keeping them ignorant.

Is it likely that the surroundings of a miserable edifice will be beautified? Who will ever be stimulated to improve the appearance of a countryside, so long as its edifices are nothing but board boxes? As one goes about in the country he is now greeted with numberless shoddy silos of wood that lean toward every point of the compass. Of late we begin to see silos of masonry as they are always constructed in France. When so built they give an air of permanence and dignity to the countryside. Of what use are our splendid new roads, constructed and projected, if they are to pass by sham wooden copies of a stronger and more honest age? Already the majority of the old Connecticut houses have been decked out with jigsaw piazzas and similar efforts, ignorantly meant for improvements. Many of the finest dwellings in America have been ruined in this way. Our public schools are doing a little by placing photographs of good architecture on their walls. If some of the time wasted in algebra and music on children who will never use either, were given to pointing out what was honest and durable and useful in architecture, some good might be accomplished.

In connection with the question of roads we notice a wholesale destruction of grand trees with a century of growth, for the sake of broadening a road perhaps a foot or two. The engineer without the love of beauty should be banished because what he destroys, under the false plea of necessity, cannot be restored for generations. There is a mania for the destruction of trees. Perhaps the high price of fuel has brought on this disease. Whatever the cause of it, the custom must be fought with all the energy of which we are capable. This is especially true because much of the wood obtained by this destruction is of slight value.

A GOOD OLD HOME

THE Webb House at Wethersfield, which used to be called Hospitality Hall, a name of which any family might be proud, is a fine example of its period, 1752. Here Washington states in his diary that he remained at one time for five days planning, with the French, the campaign of Yorktown which resulted in the victory of American arms and the end of the Revolutionary War. In the picture shown on page 147 at the bottom, the chamber nearest the beholder was that occupied by Washington. It has upon its walls now, we have reason to believe,

HAMILTON HOLT KITCHEN — WOODSTOCK

NEGLECTED BEAUTY — WINSTED

PLAY AFTER WORK—NORFOLK

BROOKFIELD BANKS

the same paper which covered it at the time he used the room. At the opposite end of the house, downstairs in front, is the room, the interior of which is shown at the top of page 148, where the conference went forward. While the porch of this dwelling was added somewhat after the time of the house, the other features are substantially original. The author expended a large labor of love upon this house, when it was in his hands, before the great war, and tried faithfully to bring things back to their original condition so far as possible. One of our patriotic societies has now taken over the property and, aside from the danger of fire, it is likely to be preserved for a long time, as perhaps the most interesting historical memorial in the state. The stone house at Guilford is so largely new that not much beyond its wonderful chimney has interest for us. But the Webb House, in its vast attic, in its fine stair, in its beautiful old parlors, its pleasant garden and its general atmosphere of home is impressive. When we add to these features the historic associations of the dwelling, it becomes a shrine and a monument. It has seemed fitting to show a considerable number of aspects of this house, which the author can the more readily do, as his interest in it is now merely Platonic. Its kitchen and kitchen chamber, shown on page 151, are each intensely interesting in their way.

A Leanto among Blossoms, as seen on page 155, exhibits a dwelling that appeals strongly to the present generation. While the leanto was in rare instances original, it was generally an addition, and was coincident with the increase of the numbers or the wealth of the family. A great many such dwellings of the eighteenth century still remain.

About East Hartford there are a good many artistic compositions on the streams and highways. We have thought fit to show one picture of Commercial Connecticut, as it exhibits pretty well the industries of the century past. The stream here shows three dams like successive steps, a bridge, and industrial buildings of various additions, all decorated with good old trees and enlivened by the dash of the waters which seem to delight in the power which they have generated, and to rejoice also as they toss their white arms and rush on toward the sea. The progress of water through its forms is no mean simile of mind and spirit as well as of matter. The water, changing its form, is sometimes a swift current, sometimes foam, sometimes a long sea wave, sometimes invisible vapor, sometimes storm cloud on its way back to the highlands and the mill. But in every form it is indestructible, following law, purpose and beauty.

PSYCHOLOGY OF ATTRACTIVENESS

HUMAN creatures seem to delight more in processes than in conclusions. The apple in the blossom is far more pleasing than in the fruit. Is this a permanent state of human minds? An exquisite composition of a roadside apple tree with splendid fruit finds, when done in a picture, no admirers, whereas the same tree, when pink and white, will cause ecstasies. We incline to the belief that the eye of the farmer looks at these things from a different standpoint from that of the artist. He is, however, sufficiently practical to believe that there is no sight more beautiful than that of a full bearing orchard hung heavily with great, luscious, blushing fruit. We take the same view of a cornfield in harvest, but there again the public seems to disagree, for it has no use whatever for pictures of the ripened corn. Is it that we love processes, because we engage in them, and care less for finished creations, because we can do nothing more with them? Baskets of fruit used to be popular on the walls of dining rooms, but is not fruit on the tree far more beautiful? We have studied, always with interest, and sometimes with exasperation, and at other times with amusement, the public tastes. Through long experience we think we know what people like. That is far from saying that they approve the most excellent things. Fashion has something to do with the matter; feeling and associations enter into the question. Does the beholder, however, often determine the value of a composition purely on the matter of its lines of beauty?

BACK FIELD BEAUTY — KENT

A DEEP RIVER COVE

A BROOKFIELD HALL

AN ABANDONED ROAD—BROOKLYN

We are prepared to make a statement which we believe will be met with some surprise: a generalization made from a very wide experience proves that the learned and the ignorant usually admire the same composition. A poor colored boy will choose the same picture that is selected by a person of the highest cultivation and largest means. Does this not prove that there is an inherent attraction aside from artistic merit? Or does it possibly prove that pictures are chosen for sentiment? Undoubtedly pictures are chosen from the general impressions that they convey rather than from careful analysis.

Another general statement is probably true: the pleasing and blossomy stage of life is chosen rather than the grand, the awful and the sublime. The appeal of sublimity reaches the few. The beauty in sublimity is not visible except as one has imagination, or a strong masculine spirit.

It is, however, easier to ask a question about art than to answer it and there is always room for " a splendid row." Why, for instance, does the water pouring over a mill wheel, as on page 68, excite far less interest than the same water in a placid lake, as on page 143?

There are those who say that life is always interesting, but we are able to say definitely that a picture containing animals, is not so well liked as a picture of still life. There is an occasional exception in favor of a flock of sheep, when the sheep are not too numerous. Not one in a thousand, however, cares for pictures of cattle, and not one in a hundred thousand cares for pictures of horses. The reader may suppose that this generalization is too dogmatic, but we are basing these remarks upon too many instances to be mistaken.

A garden might be thought to be an object of great interest, but it is one of a thousand who will choose a picture of a garden, and if a human figure is present in that garden, only one in ten thousand will choose it. These curious likings have always been a pleasing study to the writer. He confesses to a great and lasting love for many a composition at which the public never looks twice, and to a very small opinion of many themes over which the public is enthusiastic. Of course, he thinks he is right, and is willing to give a reason for the faith that is in him. Those who truly believe anything strongly, are prepared to defend it. But beauty is a subtle, abstruse and, ultimately, an indefinable idea. It is on this very account that we love to attempt its definition, and return to the effort the more eagerly after every failure. The various essays and philosophical discussions of abstract or concrete beauty have never settled upon an unvarying law in regard to it. It cannot be defined with precision, nor can it be set forth in a mathematical formula. Its reality is none the less certain, in fact, a great part of its charm must lie in its mystery, its illusiveness, its comparisons with other forms. One would say, for instance, that the sheep at the manger, on page 88, would be extremely popular. That, however, is not the case. A thousand times as many persons would choose the sheep at pasture, on page 143. In the former case we have fine details and see clearly the darling lambs. In the latter case the sheep are distant and impersonal.

Why is it, again, that a small dwelling, even a one story cottage of two rooms bowered in trees, as are several examples in this volume, should appeal a thousand times more than a stately dwelling, no matter how beautifully set? Is it because there are a thousand persons who live in a cottage to one who lives in a mansion? We think it is not the answer, for the resident of the mansion also chooses the picture of the cottage. Here the reason probably lies in the sense of coziness and intimacy with nature which a small dwelling exhibits.

Why is it again that we love pictures of forest drives and sylvan nooks but cannot be persuaded to live in the midst of such surroundings? The social student will answer that retirement, in a dwelling, is not popular; and the sanitary student will say that dwellings in the forest are damp. We believe the reason to lie in heredity. People have dwelt for countless ages huddled together for protection, and ten generations make a small impression upon the vast influence of countless years. Formerly there was fear in the forest, except for the brigand, who for his part, of course, avoided a fixed dwelling.

WATER SPRITES' LADDER—KENT

Again, one might suppose, from the admiration voiced through criticism, that the average man envies a high and stately location, with a fine residence. We do not, however, in fact, find that the average man sacrifices to obtain such a location for his family. He chooses his home for his back door neighbors, rather than for his view and his approach. Perhaps he is right. Certainly much is to be said for his choice. At any rate there is left for those who love the high and fine sites, such places as that we have titled Stately Old Connecticut, on page 176.

FLOWERS IN THE GRASS

MUCH has been said of the worship of the Japanese cherry blossoms by the people of Nippon. It is a question whether the devotion of the Hollander to his tulips is not as devout. A study of motives in carving has brought out the fact that a greater part of the carved furniture in America, made all of it, of course, in the Pilgrim century, has upon it, in some form, the tulip motive. Beyond that, the tulip was used in painted decoration in central southern Connecticut, to no small extent, about the year 1700. This tulip motive, coming directly from Holland, is an interesting side light, indicating that a great part of the art inspiration of that period in America came from the continent. This was in spite of the fact that the Pilgrims of Plymouth seemed to have brought over no carving motives, except the saw-tooth molding. New Amsterdam was thoroughly permeated with the Dutch decorations in painting, if not in carving. Of course, whatever carving they did, is also traced directly to the same origin. The special interest to us, in the whole matter, is the almost slavish restriction of that inspiration to the tulip motive. The Hollander cultivates the tulip very much as he eats and sleeps. It is a part of his constitution. The origin of this cultivation is perhaps prehistoric. We cannot doubt that the tulip is the state flower of Holland, because it appears on the hearts if not on the armorial bearings of its people. Curiously, however, it is found also imitated in iron, and such an imitation, in the form of a door latch, is in the hands of the writer.

The state flower of Connecticut is the laurel, though possibly it is not more common in that state than in Massachusetts and New York, and perhaps in other regions.

All this is prefatory to the fact that, however rare a certain flower may be in one part of the world, there is another part in which it grows wild. Where that natural growth occurs, we find the best countryside decorations. We never could half enjoy the formal rows of flowers in gardens, and we sympathize with certain sorts of shy blossoms, like the laurel, that does best when let alone, and allowed to choose its own habitat. We place the tulips in the grass of lawns because it has come to be seen, by some persons, that a flower blooming amongst grasses is more beautiful than elsewhere. The most exquisite floral decorations of Connecticut are, of course, to be seen where they spring up of themselves in the highlands, by the old fences, by the borders of a wood, or along stream banks. Above all, perhaps, the dandelion is the greatest natural agent of decoration in our part of America. In some fields it is so abundant that there is no more than enough grass visible to give it a setting. On the side roads, it even finds its place between the wheel tracks. It is so thoroughly at home that we feel it to be the most prominent and persistent native American, whatever its origin. Coming as it does in the early spring, it clothes an entire landscape with its gorgeous color, and rejoices the heart of man. While it is classified as a weed, it has certainly a peculiar merit in this respect, that it is a decoration, a food and a medicine. It is our tulip in the grass. We have referred already to the splendid fields of daisies and buttercups, and to the heads of the herd's-grass which, in its prime, is as decorative and beautiful as the exotic pampas grass.

All these flowers, classed as weeds and little thought of, are a great

THE MEETING OF MINDS—POMFRET

"IS THE FIRE READY?"

CREEK BANKS IN SPRING

A NEW ENGLAND COMMON—WOODSTOCK

part of the life of the year, almost as important to feed the heart, through the eye, as is the oxygen we breathe and the water we drink. But what shall we say of the humble and supposedly delicate violet, amongst fields of which we have repeatedly wandered in this very month of May, where we could not put down a foot without crushing its dainty blossom? On one occasion, the field was strewn with petals from a neighboring orchard so that, between the soft shell pink of apple petals and the violet tints, there was a vast fabric of dotted and intermingled color which gave an astonishing sense of the wealth of nature, and her sense of beauty. In obtaining a picture which we called "Strawberry Bank," there was nowhere a standing place except on the strawberry blooms. The soil seemed to be mostly sand. It lay in an uncared for back lot, under splendid creek side trees. Truly the spring in Connecticut has spread abroad her enchantments, and made a net for the feet of the most cynical and morose, who cannot but meditate, standing amid the blossoms, on that marvelous and undying impulse in the earth to decorate itself with the utmost splendor from year to year. No sooner is the snow mantle gone, than the green and the white, the yellow and the lavender, the pink and the blue, succeed each other across the vales, and sweeping up into the hills, penetrate the woodland paths. Even the whitewood tree puts forth its tulip blossom, hung higher in the heavens than any comparable flower. It was so ordinary a growth in Connecticut that it became, as it is yet, a commercial timber. While the tulip is the king of trees so far as its flower is concerned, the dogwood exceeds it in the lavish, indeed the complete white or pink splendor which it lifts steadily to the sky. The maple, so brilliant in the lowlands with its spring reds, follows at once with flowers which, while not full of color, are exquisite in form. So that, from the first fur on the catkins to the last blaze of the October maple, the wildwood is always embellishing itself. No receptive person can fail to be impressed with this urge and aspiration in the natural world to put forth beauty. Nor do we need to confine ourselves to the flower alone, for the leaf remains with us longer, and whether in the great spreading veins of the basswood, the long glossy oak serrations, the maple or the pine, or the sprig of hemlock with its lighter green tip, the entire out-of-doors is teeming, radiant, hopeful and prophetic of eternal beauty. From the hare bell to the huge conifer, through the entire gamut of the natural world, there is a persistent and limitless declaration that beauty is at the heart of things, and that nothing can stop its upcoming and ongoing. It says to us, in the grasses and in the oaks: " You cannot put us down; pests cannot destroy us. We are cut down and removed, but we return. For every fading there is a fuller blooming. We are going on and on. We shall cover the earth whether you will or no. Beauty is in our hearts and we must show it or die and, if we die, others will show it still more fully."

Yes, the flowers in the grass, and the flowers of the grass itself, and the blossoms that even float upon the water and are wafted in the wind, fill the earth with delight. They blow, they run, they root, in state after state, from continent to continent. By bulb, by winged maple, by feathered dandelion, even by spurs or viscous fluid that clings to our garments as we pass, they spread, and every weed is a flower. We have mentioned the endless decorative forms of snowflakes and of frost flowers. It is thus that, even in the cold and the darkness, the beauty of the world insists on expressing itself. Even in the depths, the rocks themselves take crystal shapes, and in the mud the pearl grows lustrous, and in the harbors the sea anemone opens and closes its mystery of gorgeous tints. As if this were not enough to impress us with the optimism of the universe, we cannot look up without perceiving cloud forms of magnificent and untold myriads of shapes, each with its delicate shading, from the most evanescent pearl white to the splendor of scarlet, and the deepest wealth of purple. And when the clouds pass, there is the shaded blue, sweet, calm, deep, ever dependable.

Nor in the night does beauty pass away, but in her garment of radiance, self-illuminated, she covers the earth with glory, and we cannot imagine a distance in space too great to be filled with colors

A BRIGHT CORNER—EAST HAMPTON

OLD HOMES, OLD TREES—WETHERSFIELD

MERIDEN'S LAKE

RIVULET FARM — NEWFIELDS

and forms and movements inexpressibly exquisite. The stones themselves, self-polished or wrought by the lapidary, catch up a thousand shades of beauty. We cannot go so deeply into the earth that we fail to find exquisite forms. We are familiar now with that greatest modern chemical triumph, the reproduction for us of every color hidden away by the sun in the coal seams unknown ages gone.

Even the sea, in all its moods, is splendid even when it is fearful, and there is no mountain peak so lofty as to escape a color scheme as varied as the days and the seasons. Whether we glance admiringly at the rainbow trout darting into the shadows, or at the cactus blossoms in the desert, or at the opalescent tints that come from the mines, we are met everywhere and always by something to delight. The man who is bored, is either a fool or a knave. Having eyes and nostrils and fingers we are not restricted to the admiration of a single shape or odor or color, but we may gather to ourselves, as the great clearing house of nature, all the splendors, mutations and suggestions of a universe. In the little cameras slightly more than an inch in focus, which we call eyes, we carry with us, not one, but two interpreters of creation. We cannot open our eyes without visions of splendor. We cannot prevent photography upon the brain, of a moving picture, without tawdriness, without price, a continuous performance, since the morning stars sang together.

In view of these truths, the fear expressed now and then that the world will grow ugly is, of course, overcome. Here and there war and commerce devastate and mutilate beauty, but hate and greed, which seem so persistent, are very temporary motives compared with that endless determination of the cosmos to be glorious. The battlefields are again covered with the color of glory even though it springs from the blood of men. Men, who came from the cosmos, cannot kill it. They must learn to harmonize with it, whether they will or no. If they can get into step with the march of the world, and can learn the tunes that play in the treetops and over the waves, if they can at last awake to

accord themselves with all the ongoing things, they cannot possibly fail
of their heaven, now or ever. To be alive is to be endowed with
fellowship, and to have fellowship is to partake of every good, and
every good is enough to build up a superb and satisfactory and enduring
character. When we all begin to study the assonance of language and
its capabilities of expression, we shall gather up into the style of our
speech the crystallized merits of all that has been said or sung. And
when we all set ourselves to it, we shall, with the colors available to us,
and the fibres that we may twist, form fabrics such that life and love,
poetry and history, shall appear in them. Science consists in reading
the universe as it is. Religion is in picturing it when freed from the
trammels of hate. There can be no honest religion out of accord with
the cosmos, and there can be no science contrary to absolute beauty.
The longer one wanders over the fields, the longer one climbs the mountains and sails the sea, the deeper will be his sense of his own oneness
with, and his joy in, this best possible of worlds. Strictly speaking it
is not necessary for us to try to make the world better. That would
be gilding the lily or blazoning a star. Properly, we have merely to
get out of the way, and to run with the laws of truth. Properly, we
have only to perceive that the celestial is circumambient. In the little
flower, or the small experience, we learn the universality of good. So
thought of pain is merely a lack of adjustment to law, and dullness is
a lack of perception of what is in the world.

The calamity that befalls the individual who shuts himself ever within
walls, and looks only at a machine and allows himself to be unaware
of the world he lives in, is the only real calamity. Fear is based upon
a partial view and poverty arises out of unappreciativeness. What can
we lose when even a shade of color buried for a million years cannot
be lost and when a tint of vapor will come again in the western sky,
despite the howling of all the mobs that ever rose? You cannot any
more get rid of good, in any form, however small, than you can wipe
the whole universe into nothingness. The broad view and the long

ELM LUXURIANCE — DANBURY

GRANDFATHER'S — EAST HADDAM

HILL FARM ELMS — BROOKLYN

A GLASTONBURY SPRING

view overcomes all fears and all littleness. There is not only enough for all but more than all. Whatever is scant in the world, is so because we do not need it. Nations may have grown great without diamonds but never without oxygen. The glory of high passion is capable of fusing every form into harmony. To the scientist there is no such thing as dirt or waste. We need everything in man and nature, and even the power to hate is also the power to love, when it is shot through by white light and aimed by the truth. We will say that some time Connecticut showed none of its brownstone hill-stairs, none of its flora and fauna. These possibilities slept. They were under the surface or they were in the sun. But they came out. They have unrolled themselves. They have spread their glory, their charm, their variety, their richness abroad. Shall we imagine that what was once sedimentary rock or uniform marsh, and has now become a proud state, has gone half way toward its development? Shall we be so lame in our perceptions as not to know that all that we have done, and all that we have seen, is a mere beginning? Who shall stop the movement of moisture and the chemistry of the skies? What can prevent evolution? We have traveled in a generation from protoplasm to the finest manhood that exists today in Connecticut. Will the carping and the faithless give us time for the growth of a country? Has anyone computed the relative bulk of the human knowledge, accumulated during the past two hundred years, with all that which preceded it? Now that the arms of thought are strengthened and lengthened by printing and electricity, what may we hope to make of a forward looking man and a forward looking state in the next three hundred years of American life?

THE LOVE OF VARIATION

WE have been speaking of the tulip tree as bearing a flower so near like the true tulip as to deserve the name. It is a remarkable, yet not an unique instance of the love found in nature for slight variations. It is as if, in this case, the thought had been to carry out in flowers what the classic country bumpkin wished in relation to the pumpkin. It would have been so much better, he thought, had the pumpkin grown on a tree, until the apple falling on his nose made him glad it was not a pumpkin. Nature obviously dislikes a hiatus. She desires that the mind and the eye shall be led along by gradual mutations in form, by which one flower varies slightly from another, until, after twenty such gradations, we find ourselves looking at a beautiful creation which is wholly different from the first specimen in the series. We have noticed that the snow crystal while usually six-sided, sometimes appears as a triangle. The trillium also, with its three leaves, may be matched with various flowers somewhat similar, with four, five and six leaves. The cucumber shows only two leaves at first, and some plants seem to restrict themselves to one leaf. But in the daisy, the dandelion, the aster and the rose we find a multitude of petals, until it seems that the intention was to offer an unlimited range of beautiful combinations. The same remark applies to colors in flowers, which are sometimes painted in solid masses, sometimes in shadings, and again with spots or lines in forms that lead on our imagination. This variety is not restricted to the blossom or the leaf but some flowers blend the blossom and the leaf, like the cacti, and in others the leaf itself is the chief decoration. The same variety applies to the size of vegetable growth. There are weeds that bear no slight resemblance to an elm, and others that remind us of the oak. We may find, in our dozen box of tomato plants, a little weed which suggests the beginning of the sequoia gigantea. Of course, the comparison is obvious between the

THEY GREW IN BEAUTY SIDE BY SIDE—WINSTED

A PALLADIAN GABLE—MIDDLE HADDAM

A MAY CURVE — GRISWOLDVILLE

HIGHLANDS OF THE CONNECTICUT — CHATHAM

marvels of the microscopic and telescopic worlds. It is as if the scheme of creation were arranged to suit all tastes, and to prevent the possibility of the loss of interest in any man regarding his environment. Thus it is, of course, only the superficial, who, touring about a quiet state like Connecticut, will speak disparagingly of its moderate elevations. Nevertheless we recognize that there are persons who can see beauty only in lofty mountains, just as others are interested only in the sea. This narrowness of interest may be disastrous to a life. It is always impoverishing.

There is also an intense pleasure in observing the growth and change in an individual plant or flower. The process from the hidden bud through its opening into fulness of bloom and at last into fruitage is really the unveiling before us of a life process. It is certain that one who can see nothing good in a miniature, cannot see all that there is in a mastodon. That inscrutable mystery of human likings also interests us. Thus one housewife confines her attention to roses. Another finds a stronger appeal in the less modest peony. But in every form of life there are lines of beauty. In the serpent we are so overwhelmed by our natural repugnance that we forget the grace in the horror. The same may be true of the sea in its wildest moods. But the ugliest animal has its movements or contours of grace, and there is nothing created that does not appeal, at least at some time in its development or in some phase of its action, to our sense of beauty.

As if this were not enough, we have not been satisfied with the achievements of nature, but have set ourselves, by crossings and cultivation, to bring out new forms. While Burbank removes the thorn from the cactus, a grower of orchids develops a new shape and gives it a name, so that flower lovers all over the world bid madly for specimens. We remember in the days of boyhood an extravaganza in the form of an essay on the call of the west, in which the writer spoke of bread from the bread tree and butter from the butter tree. It was only one more indication that we are like the natural world in our desire to modify still further the methods of creation. In spite of the luxuriant provisions of unassisted nature, we have developed the potato from a mere marble, and the wheat grain from a very inferior wild variety. It is this agreement of our own feeling with the urge found in nature that thrills us the more with joy in observing and working with nature. The old world artist, whose reproductions in glass of so many thousand forms are now found in the Peabody Museum, finds a minor counterpart in every one of us. The artist is busy in copying the flowers and the clouds and every form that appeals to him particularly. The sculptor was, perhaps, the first artist. The architect decorated his constructions with floral motives after he had imitated the great trees in his columns. Even now rustic furniture is liked by many because it is so near to nature. The so-called new art among the French seeks to use, as far as possible, every natural line in flowers and trees. There is not a manufacturer, from a piece of fretted iron to the inwrought leaves on Irish linen, that does not seek to copy or improve upon nature, and in every nation, nearly, a national flower has been blended with the arts and artisanship of its people, until in many cases it has exhibited a certain happy and apparently inevitable consonance with the object a part of which it has become. Thus the thistle, the rose, the fleur-de-lis, and as many others as one cares to think of, have entered into the lives of the nations which have made much of them. We cannot go back to a period so early that the lotus, or the acanthus, or the reed, or some blossom or growth does not form a part of a national tradition, or worship or art development. This immense variety sometimes results in variations which fill a seemingly necessary need, or at any rate become a great convenience. We may be sure that for every successfully developed motive there have been many failures. Thus in the work of Chippendale, his immensely discursive imagination ranged from China to Italy, and in the course of his career he tried out as many motives as he could possibly find time to do. Practically, the taste of his patrons and imitators has lighted upon certain of his motives as being apt and

A BLOSSOMY SHORE—CHESTERFIELD

CONNECTICUT IN SPRING—EAST HARTFORD

THE TURN OF THE CREEK—EAST HARTFORD

THE POND IN MAY—SOUTH WINDSOR

charming and wholly desirable; whereas others of his motives, however fashionable they were for a time, have fallen into disuse and even abuse, a fate not always undeserved. It is as if this notable artificer had a pride in showing how many forms he could create, and in throwing them forth to the public to take their choice. He is really only one among many workers, all of whom have sought to add something different to the stock of human achievement. At times, however, certain nations have shut themselves up more and more to a limited number of forms, or they have, in certain ages, followed one type. So shut-in nationalities, like China and Japan, develop to the last possible degree certain art motives. The world is really the richer for this narrow and deep culture, for it has produced perfection in its kind, and some of the nations following the same tendency in developing another motive have contributed their share for human use. One never ceases to marvel at the apparently slavish devotion to the Gothic in northern Europe through several centuries. But the moment one looks at all beneath the surface, one sees that a continuous development of the Gothic was proceeding, so that a close student may detect sometimes a variation of twenty years in style. The sum total of these variations is legion, yet through all of them there is a central trend which makes them Gothic.

It has been supposed by some that the failure to make innovations is a mark of the lack of progress. This conclusion may be fallacious. Possibly the taste of the artist is only becoming more severe and more precise, and that he is carrying to perfection some of his lines. It is by this twin capacity of human nature, the perfection of form, and the development of variety, that the world is enriched, and that man has shown his unity with the natural world. We find, for instance, that certain orders of animal life have not changed perceptibly through untold geologic ages, while other forms of life seem to be in a process of rapid mutation. It is not a smaller world that we are learning to envision. We do see statements that the world is growing smaller, but any man who has sought to learn the whole of any one subject knows that the bounds of the world are infinite.

Now this love of variation sometimes shows itself in forms of good taste, as in a garden one may have a large number of flowers somewhat alike. But the old-fashioned nosegay which contained one each of as great a number of flowers as possible we feel to be in poor taste, and we prefer to make up a vase of flowers all of one variety or at most of flowers backed by greenery. The same principle applies in all art. The mixing of several orders of architecture in one edifice is distasteful, as the mixture of many periods of furniture in one room is distasteful. That is to say we find that the love of variety should proceed according to a certain law. Can we define that law? Broadly, there requires, of course, to be harmony of color or line and nothing in a group, a room, or an edifice, that is distracting. The pulling of the mind from one form to something unrelated to it is a strain very much like the effort to see two things at once. That is to say, a general law may be laid down to the effect that our human compositions should avoid bizarre effects, or anything that savors of an attempt to bring the ends of the earth together. A single object cannot be too beautiful, too rich or too perfect. But a medley, even of perfect things, that are not related by some general motive, is disturbing to a cultivated taste.

In this connection we notice that nature takes many liberties which we dare not imitate. Certain cloud colorings or groupings of blossoms, which are not offensive as we find them in nature, would not answer for us to incorporate in a single decorative scheme. We are not yet great enough, or sufficient masters of the secrets of universal composition, to attempt some things which are mere child's play for nature. It is on this account that, while we are novices, we are in danger of lack of restraint, and, by attempting all, to accomplish worse than nothing. The decorative work of an American Indian escapes this fault because, owing to the limitation of his materials, or the narrowness of his traditions, he kept to one line sufficiently to produce artistic results. The artist or the

DOWN TO THE LAKE—MIDDLEBURY

A CORNWALL WAYSIDE

THE SHAKEN MIRROR—MIDDLESEX COUNTY

WATER STAIRS—KENT

artisan may take up the tools of his trade, and say, " Am I not free? May I not do what I will with my own? " He does not yet know that all creation is subject to the severest law, which he must, either consciously or otherwise, follow in order to produce anything worth while. Thus the nineteenth century builders, following the love for new forms, insisted upon the incorporation of incongruous shapes just because they were new, and not because they were good. They did not try first to apply severe canons of taste to their designs. They incorporated in their work any freak or fancy that came to them. Thus the love of variety in painting has brought havoc and, at times and places, has brought art itself into ridicule.

We may then deduce another general law of variation: we should avoid the grotesque and the unseemly as nature does.

As we pass through the various valleys of Connecticut we see in each some one feature which seems carried to its best estate. Tobacco grows to its perfection in one section, corn in another section, potatoes in a third. The elm tree arrives at its most wonderful majesty in the Connecticut valley; the buttonwood seems to flourish in most luxuriance on the lower Housatonic; the willow is dominant on the upper Housatonic; the hill orchards to the east of the Connecticut seem perfect for peaches. There is a time and a place at which every growth reaches its highest form. While many sorts of trees and flowers appear in fine development over wide areas there are others that are very timid and restricted. We do not find many fine birches in Connecticut except in the highlands. Care and selection has developed the cut leaf birch so that specimens on lawns appear in great beauty. But in the wild state they are not in evidence.

Every district should take care to assist the development and preservation of those particular forms of vegetation that tend to perfect themselves there. In this way the sublimity of certain noble trees may set a mark for our imagination, and the coloring and contour of certain flowers may easily be induced to exhibit themselves at their best.

We should say, therefore, that, as the third general law, we should

first foster the perfect growth of the normal form of a plant, to establish
a high and splendid standard. We may then go on to experiment in the
development of varieties. Thus it is, where the elm appears normally
in its utmost majesty, that we are most likely to find the feathered elm,
the weeping elm, the elm with imbricated leaves, the vase elm and the
oak shaped elm, and the elm with " the friendly crook."

Only a slight study of the flora of Connecticut is required to discover
various forms which are at their best in this state, and which afford us
endless pleasure in developing them from sports and crosses.

PRIVATE DRIVES

SKIRTING the Arrowana, page 179, is a good example of a private
drive. Following a fine stream it connects the public highway with
the residence, perhaps a quarter of a mile distant. There is a sidewalk
of flagstones which adds very much to the composition. The road is
the more interesting because it is not too carefully trimmed at the sides.
A gravel road of this sort where the grass is allowed to trespass a little
irregularly, is far more pleasing and far less expensive. The same
condition obtaining, all over the world, of the difficulty of securing good
country labor, is found by many millionaires who cannot keep up their
estates as they would keep up a city place. Perhaps this pinch may teach
us how to get beauty out of country places without employing so many
people upon them.

An apple tree at the entrance to a drive by the side of the gate also
supplies an interesting beginning. This same drive a little farther on is
seen in " An Alluring Road."

At the bottom of page 223 we get the good effect of a gable facing
one on entering a home drive. In this case we have an arched window
with narrow flanking side windows. The picket fence is the next thing
in attractiveness for a country place, after a stone wall.

HOMESTEAD BLOSSOMS—NEWFIELDS

STRAWBERRY BANK—MERIDEN

MUSICAL WATERS

An entrance under great elms, as on page 215, is always attractive. It takes a long time to secure a row of trees and if one is arranging a drive one can frequently lead it between or by the side of fine trees already grown, giving all the effect of great age and dignity. In fact, it is by such accommodations rather than by new work that the best results are obtained. Anybody can arrange a country place so that its drive will be dignified five hundred years from now, but there is an immense pleasure in reaching successful results through the material already at hand.

The Abandoned Road, on page 204, is really another private drive in delightful Brooklyn. It is now well overgrown with grass, only a faint path being left. There is an occasional break in the row of trees, not yet filled in. We have no doubt that in process of time the sense of aesthetic value will cause such old drives to be preserved carefully.

It is fine to be greeted at the gate by blossoms, as on page 188. The effect is none the worse because the gate is gone. In fact, we think the effect on the visitor is fine, for, turn it as we will, we can never get over the feeling that a gate is inhospitable. We must needs trespass to go through it to inquire if we may go through it!

Of course it is a privilege merely to be alive in the spring and to enter at such a drive as that on page 171. It is not a wonder that a youth born here went out to make his place in the scholastic world. Where nature herself is eloquent and sympathetic and beautiful, she supplies at least half of our education.

We are reminded by the picture of a forest drive on page 167 of the usual meaning of a forest in England. It is open glades with here and there a clump of trees or a large lone tree, that give woodland its greatest charm. A poet has stated that the groves were God's first temples. Probably he referred to the cult of the Druids. At any rate, whether his supposition is correct, it is certain that the modern camp meeting has sought the grove. We remember a childhood experience of attending such a camp meeting among the birches and the maples. The porches of the dwellings were built of birch, and the sunshine playing on the salmon bark through the twinkling leaves was a part of our memory. We are sorry that we cannot say we believe trees make people good, but we do believe that trees help in that direction. They are so honest and sturdy and so sympathetic that they must make their appeal.

We wonder what the effect of motors will be on the country drives of Scotland where sheep roam at will. What can be more satisfactory than driving along among sheep that know no fear and past deer that seem to themselves safe when only a few rods distant? We have yet much to learn since we in America, at least, almost never admit sheep in private grounds. We seem to love, better, untrained dogs, roaming at will to slaughter or harry the home flock.

How much we wish to know what lies up the cart path on page 135. We must walk or we shall crush the petals that have gathered in the ruts. We wonder wouldn't it be a good thing to fill all ruts with petals? The mystery of what is beyond might be thought to be sufficiently impenetrable without creating mysteries in curves like these. But, as a matter of fact, we love mystery. Children in their play seek to be mysterious. What is a novel without mystery? Or a mine? Or a trout pool? Or the morning mail? We are creatures so intrigued by mystery that we create it where it does not exist. We like to throw a gossamer veil over our theology even, and what politician is there who is not mysterious? Who at the present time really knows what are the policies of political parties in America, or in England, for that matter? And who wants to know? We make a good pretense of calling forth the other side, but all the fun is in surprises, and we are bound to admit that there is a good deal of fun. A large part of the charm of an old house is its mystery, and who is there who would not pay a considerable advance for an old country place that was haunted? All you have to do is to point out a passage behind a chimney, or a secret drawer in a desk, and at once everybody is delighted. We care more for such things than we do for what we can see clearly, however important that may be.

In fact, this playing with mystery in the curves of roads such as that

A LITTLE BAY—MANCHESTER

CREST COTTAGE—SALEM

A GATE OF JOY—GRISWOLDVILLE

THE HEART OF THE WOOD—MIDDLETOWN

on page 119 or 120, is merely a reflex of a fundamental trait. Life would be appalling had it not many disclosures to make to us. A future with nothing to learn, and even a past that we can thoroughly understand are the essence of boredom. If you know what is in the old chest and what is behind the apparent, and if you can analyze the sunset, life becomes as dry as dust.

No, we did not go to the end of a lane in Norwichtown, page 91. We have it in store for us to know what is beyond the curve. It would be a calamity if there were no new roads to follow.

The life of the inventor always has an intense zest because he is at the borders of knowledge which has been hidden from the foundation of the world. He has caught the hem of Minerva's skirt, and he will not let go until she helps him in his quest. But what a poor creature he would be if the answer to his question satisfied him?

As Edison did not stop after his first invention, so any boy who asks a question wants to know something else or there would be no hope for young America. The thing that stopped human progress for ages was fear, or possibly religious awe, about launching out into the great deep to learn what was beyond. The maps were peopled with uncouth and horrible monsters to indicate that one must pass far beyond the Gates of Hercules or beyond the bounds of Scythia. All religious dry rot has been caused by the effort to hinder the investigation of mysteries. It is only a very limited intelligence that does not understand how the opening of one mystery merely leads to the gate of another. Any kind of progress is brought about by a reverent knocking at some hitherto unopened gate. Any large soul will understand that the crossing of one ocean only brings him to the strand of some greater sea. So the discoverer of the Pacific crossed the isthmus and behold, that wider ocean opened on his charmed gaze! We believe that the astronomers have lately completed a map of the heavens showing three million stars. They tell us that with this they have only made a beginning, since they have reached the limit of their present telescopes. They are not silly enough to imagine that all mysteries are solved or that we shall be without some curve to round, always, on our road to discover greater beauties.

Indeed, perhaps, beauty itself derives its charm mostly from its mystery. What is behind a pair of flashing eyes? Perhaps we think we know, sometimes, but do we? What is beauty but a reflection of some reality at present occult? Some would say that beauty is the reflection of light playing upon form and color. But we are told that intelligent blind people find great pleasure in passing their hands over the surface of objects. No, beauty must be something more than a reflection. As we see beauty, it is probably the gate of some greater reality.

ARE THE BEST THINGS RARE?

MORALISTS have assured us that the best things are the commonest, but we wonder whether they are not half deceived and half deceiving. Would it not be more correct to say that some good things are common? Would it not be more correct to discriminate that the elements of good are very common, but that their combinations in their highest form are rare? The individual tree of great beauty is often to be found; but in a proper setting it is not common, and in conjunction with many companions it is even rare. That is, the ideal state in which individual human beings are set properly in the natural world has hitherto been found an unattainable goal. Out of a hundred landscapes one is best. The finest combinations are rare. In a human character goodness of heart is found in one, talent in another, — yet how many Washingtons were there? In the War of 1812 where was the Washington? In the Civil War the South early discovered its Lee, but how long it took the North to discover its Grant! We should cease to be satisfied with beauty spots in the world and with the occasional great character. When every farm owner determines that his farmstead shall be an esthetic

BETWEEN THE BUTTONBALLS — NEW MILFORD

VERY DUTCH—BROOKFIELD CENTER

MOUNTAINSIDE PASTURE—KENT

center, and when every youth makes the determination of a young Washington, we shall gradually spread our good without thinning it.

Of the hundred thousand students annually trained in our colleges in the use of their mother tongue how many write well? Of all the country places in Connecticut how many would be thoroughly satisfactory to an Olmstead or a Homer? How many natural settings are there not marred by the intrusion of something unlovely?

We should, therefore, not dismiss the idealist with a shrug, and tell him that everything is as it should be. The only reason why this is the best possible world is that it is the best that strugglers after the ideal have so far been able to make it. The moment any one who sees a finer goal attainable ceases to strive after it the world becomes to him a poor sort of world. We can tolerate the present state of things only while we are conscious that we are doing everything in our power to better that state. The farmer looks out over his good hayfield, ripe to cut. It is a good world. But if he hesitates in the reaping the world, in the phrase of the street, goes bad on him. The dictum that this is the best possible of all worlds is not at all understood by a surface interpretation. The meaning, of course, is that, with the forces at work upon it, it is, at this moment, the best possible. One would entirely misread the dictum if he thought of it as predicating a satisfactory world, or a finished world. The world is like a train, satisfactory only as it keeps moving toward its destination. It is satisfactory where it is because it is going away from that place. No doubt the world is moving on schedule. It would be a blind philosophy that would suppose the world had arrived. It never will arrive for the reason that, like the German who died, it will have to go somewhere yet. These facts are encouraging to all who are true progressives It may be, indeed, that some are in a treadmill, but if they stand still they go back.

Obviously, therefore, the engineer and the playwright, although they may find perfect materials to work with, find the highest difficulty in assembling and relating their material. We remember the rich, uneducated man who put a bible in his library at the end of every fifty books, to give the thing a moral tone. Similarly we may buy a dictionary and take Shakespeare for our middle name, but how many shall we fool? It is only recently we have been informed that the ultimate particle of matter is indestructible and unchangeable. That is, it cannot wear out or suffer injury. The simplest form of material, to put this in another way, is the most perfect form. It is in combinations that we meet our difficulties and show our genius. How many ages did it take the world to utter the one phrase, "A thing of beauty is a joy forever"? Silent, inscrutable truth in the realm of ideas or the realm of physics has waited a long time, and for the most part is still waiting, till we strike the proper key for unlocking it. So we may go back thousands of years and find a finished phrase which somebody then first uttered and which has never been improved. And, looking into chemistry, we find that the ancients had dim vision or even gave leading hints of facts which have now become familiar. But the world has waited. The material is perfect; the combination that is perfect comes slowly and for the most part has not come about at all. It is said that the process of making rubber valuable was an accidental discovery of Goodyear. It is always remarkable that these accidents occur in the experience of men who are determined to know. The lightning may know where to strike better than we think. Little by little we are learning to make combinations, and he is a bigot who supposes that the world can not progress beyond a certain point. It would not be at all a bad idea for those who think the Pilgrims were stereotyped in their faith, to be told again that the chief of all the Pilgrims declared that there was much truth yet to break forth from the word of God. Perhaps some of the followers of that leader have forgotten what he said. Whether it is chemistry or religion or automobiles, none of them are any good unless they have go in them.

The joy of living, then, consists in making combinations of elemental things. That they will fit into a complete whole of beauty there can

A HILLSIDE HOMESTEAD — COVENTRY

A TUFTED PENINSULAR — MIDDLETOWN

A HIGHLAND POOL—MIDDLEBURY

MOUNTAIN SNOW—KENT

be no doubt, and if we can put together only a few of them we shall derive much pleasure from life. Of course this is a truism to some: if it were a truism to all we could have no pessimists and no discouragement; we should have no bad taste and no bad morals. So we keep saying over the same important thing, which is the burden of great literature and great life.

Human occupations may, then, be divided into efforts in various directions for combinations that will prove satisfactory. Gray is said to have spent many years upon the Elegy. We think no one regrets his not doing it more rapidly. If it took him a month to get the right word was it not a month well spent? Was it not better than a whole lifetime of bucolic mind? On the other hand some genius may dash off a great composition at a single sitting. We call it quick work, but, in reality, it is probably only the quick utterance of what has been assembling itself for forty years, like Webster's great speech, ostensibly composed in a night. In practice the easiest truth seems to come slowly and the most difficult truth to come quickly. This is simply because when we see half way through a combination, the rest of the way may be comparatively easy.

The person who first attained to the successful making of artificial silk proposed to speak of his achievements before a religious organization. The appositeness of the offer was not seen at the time. Yet here was a man who had concentrated for many years on the task of recombining the constituents of cotton so that they would have the constituents of silk. Here was a marvelous concentration which has resulted in a more marvelous dissemination. He did not at all change the elements of things. He only changed their combinations. Underlying, therefore, all efforts is always a confidence in law, a faith in the reliability and the permanence of ultimate materials. Also, stimulating all effort, is the hope that we may combine some of these materials. Combination is life. Coalescence of two particles of matter means architecture, or poetry, or whatever you will. The man who combines is a maker. He who does not combine is a dead one. He who combines wisely is a genius or a persistent worker, sometimes both. The organizing mind holds the world in the hollow of his hand. The other day they staged on the Housatonic River a miniature lightning flash, which, in its resonance and effects otherwise, was precisely similar to what we observe in the thunder storm, only on a minor scale. We are certainly getting ahead in our combinations. They tell us there are millions of horse power wasted with every lightning flash. There are millions of good effects for which human genius holds the key in the realm of beauty, of order, of creative social achievement, and maybe, some day, we shall harness a good deal more of the unused brain and muscle. One has only to stand at the door of a motion-picture house, or to walk through the great public parks, to see that the shortage of labor is a shortage of will. The casual observer would say that most people are not working. Instead of combining, they are disintegrating. And if one were to count all the men who stop work on the highway when a motor goes by, so rare a thing, he would say that most of those that are working are not accomplishing much. It would require no keen student to conclude that from four to ten times the present number of effective combinations might be made if everybody tried. That is why the world is so long in getting combed out and in arraying itself harmoniously.

The best things, therefore, are rare in proportion as they become more complex, more complete as parts of a perfected organization. We are taught that even the world does not follow a true circle in its revolutions about the sun, and it is too much to hope that we shall reach the limit in any direction soon, but the rest of life is in moving in that direction.

A CONNECTICUT CASCADE — KENT

AN ALLURING ROAD—GRISWOLDVILLE

MAY SHORES—WINDSOR

BEAUTY IN THE WATERS

SOME twenty years ago the author wrote an article on the photographic beauty of objects in motion, most of which article, as he recollects it, concerned the movement of water. Returning after so long to consider what new light experience has thrown on this subject he would say that the movement of water, or at least its surface effects, enters into a very substantial proportion of all pictorial work.

The placidity of water speaks for peace, and appeals to the minds seeking rest. Water, of course, was the first mirror, and the Greek fable of the beautiful youth who fell in love with his own image is only an allegory of water reflections, with the natural deductions. The most striking aspect of a water mirror is the consideration that nature makes its own pictures. Drops of water under certain favorable circumstances are seen to reflect the sun, and the mirage is merely a cloud reflection, cast back upon the earth. Any one may see the same thing by looking in certain lights at the dusty surface of the windshield on his motor. I was startled the other day by seeing in such a reflection water flowing through the grass. It was a combination of two true reflections put together in such a way as to deceive. The images which are found in nature of course stimulated the savage to make a record on the rock beside the stream like that which he saw within it. Practically any artist will avoid precise reflections, and will watch for hours, if necessary, for that sort of water the surface of which is touched by an evanescent wind, to provide a certain mystery and a half-veiled effect. Of course, if he is picturing the sea, he will as a rule seek its more boisterous moods, its white caps, and the spray blown from the tops of its curling, subtly-tinted breakers, or for the impact of its solid mass against the cliffs where suddenly it pales and froths and falls back from a vain assault. The movement of fresh water over natural falls as shown in various moods on page 251, and in similar sketches, has the combined charm of beauty and the impression of power. It may be an allegory on the trend of the modern world that everywhere natural falls are being harnessed and their beauty destroyed, their waters being bound to grind in the prison house of a deep-set turbine. Of course we find lofty falls only in a mountainous region which is also a region of rain. Falls are extremely rare in the arid regions of the mountains, but fairly common on the Pacific slopes. In Connecticut there are numerous highlands which afford us pleasing, rather than stupendous, waterfalls. It is, however, in the rapids of streams, or in their slight break over obstructions that their beauty for the artist more often lies. He has shown his predilection, as may be seen by going through any great gallery, for the quieter reaches of streams which merely complain at pebbles rather than roar at cliffs. It is only occasionally that we find the genius and the daring that will attempt the rainbow above the cataract, but when this is successfully done the effect is, of course, magnificent. The tufts that stand out from shallow bays, and the growths which spread themselves on the surface of the stream, are efforts at decoration which seem to say that, so far as they are concerned, decoration is the chief province of life. It is just above the mud that the water is usually most beautiful. Indeed it is in these shallows by the shore that life is said to have begun. Certainly life never forgets to teem and to make beautiful all the shallows.

It is said also that water purifies itself by aeration, and we believe that water is, for commercial purposes, artificially mixed with air by being poured over miniature cascades. It is on account of the greater air in mountain streams that the active trout prefers them. A person who has been obliged to drink boiled water from which the air is mostly banished perceives at once the flatness of the effect, and can understand how the leaping and gamy fish love to ascend through the rapids. Of course water, when as intimately connected with air as it is in the clouds, comes thereby still more beautiful, being subject to the fantastic gusts which always bring about some new combination of beauty.

DECORATIONS OF THE VALLEY — MACEDONIA

A CONNECTICUT VALE — MACEDONIA

WEDDING OF WATERS—WINDHAM COUNTY

UNCLE NATHAN'S—WETHERSFIELD

THE CHARTER OAK

THIS tree, so full of sentiment for us, blends romance and history in the most remarkable manner, perhaps, of any tree in America. It is fortunate that the Connecticut Historical Society possesses a painting of such an excellent character, a copy of which was kindly loaned for use here. We have appropriately, we think, closed the book with the picture. On another page we show a picture of the great crude chair which is also in the possession of that society. Another chair, in the legislative halls of the state, is a more finished article, and therefore has not, for us, the interest of this massive section of the old tree.

THE FALLS OF KENT

WE hope our readers may be ready to enjoy with us a Connecticut Cascade (page 251). The grouping of the hemlock bough before the fall is a touch of artistry of which only nature would be capable. The wonder of the lichen upon these rocks and their beautifully broken contours suggests to us the union of the delicate with the strong. We know no more delightful excursion than that to these falls beginning in the meadow far below and following up to the source. In that meadow by the side of the same stream we found in full effect the Annual Revival (page 271). In reviewing our impressions of the entire state we feel strongly that the section from somewhat below New Milford to a point somewhat north of Cornwall is the most pleasing of the narrower valleys of the state, more intimate than the Connecticut highlands, though each of these districts has its great and peculiar charm.

EXCURSION DAYS

WE venture upon outlining a few excursions for leisurely people who have time to look at beauty. Starting from Warehouse Point one may wander over a wide and nearly level valley, all about Broad Brook, whose placid curves and noble trees and the fair farms through which it flows may serve to hold one for hours. In the pastures by the side of some pool will be found an ideal spot for a luncheon. Wandering on, westward, past the streams and over the hills of Rockville we may approach, through Tolland or Ellington, Stafford Springs and thence Stafford. This district is marked by bold outlines of hills at the foot of which are small ponds or hurrying waters. Stafford is one of the well chosen summer resorts which appeals to the writer very strongly. A road coming into this district from Southbridge will soon bring this region into very great prominence as a beautiful country in which to rest or through which to drive. The Willimantic River, flowing south from Stafford, reveals many beauties. Crystal Lake in Ellington and Stafford has more gently sloping shores but is yet well up in the highlands. Tolland is really a mountain town, some of its crests rising to about a thousand feet or more, and its hills being charming with their rapidly changing contours. In this town Skungamaug River rises. It is a somewhat pretentious name for a small stream but its banks, in the somewhat wild districts of Covington, are worthy of following down to Andover. It is not supposed that one can cover all this ground in a day, but spending the night at Stafford Springs he may return to Hartford through Rockville if he came by Ellington. In Rockville the fine waters of the Shenipsit Lake, a broad reservoir of power, lie in great beauty amongst the hills, so that we have in Rockville an ideal location for an industrial center, a fact happily recognized by the strong men of that region, who have developed it and who are trying to make their village beautiful to match its setting.

A VILLAGE GREEN — GILDERSLEEVE

A TUFTED MEADOW — BROOKFIELD

An excursion from Pomfret may take us through the three Wood-stocks, finely typical of good early American village features, several of which we have set forth. As Woodstock is the last town we visited in the state to complete our work, so in our minds it is the town to which our thought goes back, as is proper, for the last is the best of Connecticut. South Woodstock has a pleasing green from which, however, we hope the sense of local pride may succeed in removing the poles. With its fine trees and its public edifices and a dwelling which was an old inn, it is a good example of a common. Woodstock Center has another ancient inn, now and for long the residence of the Hamilton Holts. The rambling house, part of which, in a very English way, is a grange hall and a separate property, was, of course, built at different periods as most romantic old dwellings were. The interior is elsewhere mentioned. The farm lands open beautifully at many points of the road as we pass north. One may return from Woodstock through Putnam with its fine falls (page 15), and go on to Brooklyn and thence to Pomfret. A short day but full of loveliness.

Stonington offers headquarters from which the enrapturing miniature fields, closed in with walls, may be seen in their perfection. One never tires of watching these walls as they range one behind another, seven or eight lines of them, and as they converge with an apple tree at the corners of the intersections, and as they close in the cosy home, or wander away over the distant hills. Old Mystic may be united with rambles about Stonington and in this district one would say it is better to spend a whole day, if not a dozen. There are shore drives, hill drives, and valley drives.

We have mentioned New London as a center of drives, one of the most important centers in fact. Passing thence to Norwich one may follow its valleys into the hills in three or four directions, making headquarters in this very old-fashioned district. The Congregational parsonage here is a fine example of the four chimneys, each in a corner. Located as it is on a small green, it is thoroughly satisfactory to the eye and to the feeling, and the venerable pastor is most happily housed here. Lyme, the artist's resort, being now supplied with an exhibition hall for its annual or more frequent displays, is an altogether entrancing village. Whether one goes down to Black Rock or follows the shore road past ancient houses to East Lyme and New London and thence back by the main road, or follows the small stream north to Hamburg and thence into the wildest section of Connecticut, one is sure of several memorable days. If one desires metropolitan conditions in the evening and the country in the daytime one may choose New Haven or Bridgeport as excursion centers. Stamford and Greenwich are towns surrounded by numerous stately country places where, if one has the entrée, the charms of a somewhat English neighborhood may be unveiled. Ridgefield, near the New York line, is a kind of extension of New York's Westchester district with fine, fair lands opening long vistas of winding drives.

Woodbury, with its surrounding districts, is distinctly rural and if one desires quiet, a district with bold hills and good drives, there is nothing much better. In the next town, Southbury, the author enjoyed several years, accumulating experience and the records of Connecticut landscapes. He yearns again for those quiet acres, and could ask no better old age than to return to them.

Waterbury is, of course, the large center in this region for those who wish fine appointments. North, south, east and west one finds at Watertown and toward Torrington, or on an excursion to the summit of Southington Mountain, or in a drive down the picturesque Naugatuck, or into the splendid highlands of Middlebury, quite different neighborhoods, each with a very distinct charm. We think we may have noticed sufficiently Litchfield, Norfolk, Sharon, and New Milford as resting points from which one may go out from a day to a month to become familiar with the rapid streams and the fine bold hills of the Connecticut Berkshires. Indeed, there is a village in this district named Berkshire just as one finds such a village north of Pittsfield.

Perhaps the love of seeking out loveliness may not be a passion of the

A RIVER SYCAMORE—NEW MILFORD

A CONNECTICUT CORNER—EAST HARTFORD

A FRAMED BROOK—MERIDEN

great body of tourists, but is not the varied joy of river bend or lofty downs, of dear little villages, of clumps of quiet pines or maples better than society as it is constituted?

THE BEAUTY OF OLD AGE

YOUNG people do not give much attention to the beauty of old age and it is likely that they might deny its possibility. Their elders might reply that the immature and unfinished period of youth was also lacking in beauty. Both young and old would be wrong. There is a wonderful charm about growth even when it is incomplete. To be sure there is a time when lambs and children are rather leggy and it is only the eye of the parent or the artist that can count this age beautiful. When, however, we pass to vegetation we might extract from the assurance of youth the admission that some old trees are beautiful. There is a subtle connection between age and beauty in trees. A massive bole and huge branches have a charm far superior to that exercised upon us by a young tree, however perfect it may be. The sense of antiquity associated with a wide spreading oak or elm mingles in our estimate of its beauty in a manner impossible of analysis. The association of youth and age seen when children play beneath a oak, greatly adds to the beauty of each. It is by observing this that Corot has achieved many of his finest compositions. At my door as I write, is a tree which may easily have been a seedling during the campaigns of Charlemagne. It may have been nearly as large as it is today when William conquered the English. When Columbus arrived perhaps it was larger than it is now and when Massachusetts was settled it was certainly magnificent. Its arms themselves would each make a large tree. Think of the pests it has outlived! Think of the terrific storms it has weathered! The coming and going of empires have never impressed it, but with every autumn its acorns have fallen hopefully, and with every spring its pale, first green leaves have unrolled. It is useless to tell me that it is a mere matter of sentiment to comfort myself with its steadying presence. We simply enjoy such a growth. It is no more necessary to analyze that pleasure than to analyze a kiss.

There is an elm, also, in our town, on which it is said several thousands of dollars have been expended to preserve it. If you see that tree you will say the care has not been extravagant. Thus, while it may be the few who feel the importance of preserving fine, old growths in Connecticut, we may well be assured that some time in the coming centuries the children of men will bless those who have set apart lands to be sacred forever like the classic groves of the Aegean.

Probably not a voice of protest would arise from the most practical citizen if the Charter Oak could be brought back to life at almost any cost. But if care had been given to it continuously we should have it today, perhaps.

One has only to look about a little to see how few patriarchs of the forest remain. A few vague statements picked up at random and not deemed worthy of being included in dignified histories, indicate that at the time of settlement Connecticut contained many trees of such mass and dignity that, could Connecticut have been preserved in its original state, it would now be the wonder land of America. The Indian habitation was of just about the sort fitted to preserve the finest trees, which usually grew in the open and were not interfered with. No close forest growth ever presents trees of individual beauty as they can not produce lateral branches of any size. Wherever great branches are found today we may be sure that for thousands of years there has been an open glade about the tree which bears them. In the old world they have handled these matters more carefully, and we find individual, historic trees in great numbers. In spite of the interest in such matters we can scarcely drive a mile without finding some magnificent reminder of other centuries tottering to its fall or already the victim of the axe. What is the value of a great tree? Commercially speaking, it may add one half to the worth

CONNECTICUT CLIFFS—MERIDEN

THE LITTLE HOME—GLASTONBURY

GUARDIANS OF THE SHORE—BROOKFIELD

A HOUSATONIC BOW—NEW HAVEN COUNTY

of a home which nestles by its side, but to the eye of affection it is removed from appraisal almost as much as our mistress's eyebrow. We resent the intrusion of any other estimates except those that appeal to the affections. Between the street and the field the old trees are jostled first on one side and then on another. The noblest specimens that remain to us have been injured by the highway or the sidewalk. The great Wethersfield elm is the worse for both of these intrusions. It is forgotten that roots of trees are not far below the surface. We hear about tap roots, and it is said that the walnut, in California, will send its roots many feet into the ground in search of water, and if they find it the tree with which they are connected ceases to fruit. But trees such as we know and love for their shade or even for their fruit, in the east, grow exclusively in the surface soil. No grading, therefore, can be undertaken anywhere near them. The roots of a tree extend about as far as the branches and this may be taken as a point within which no disturbance of the soil should be permitted.

It is probably true that civilization has diffused the pests that attack trees. Certainly some such pests have crossed the Atlantic as they could not have done once. It is nothing short of a miracle that a tree anywhere should have been rugged enough to withstand all adversaries for a thousand years or more. Successive years of drought weaken trees. They can bear being denuded also of leaves for one season and in rare instances for two seasons, by pests, but if they have reached a period beyond exuberant vitality they sooner or later succumb. Three vast oaks in a row stand out in my memory with blackened branches, now whitening in death. It is a surprise and a sorrow that now new conditions should bring about such devastation. An old chestnut, when flourishing, is one of the most picturesque growths of Connecticut, but just now we cannot recall any noble chestnut of our acquaintance that is not at least half dead. The pine blight, the last terrible menace, is said to forebode wide and perhaps general destruction. The saving of field crops by spraying is feasible but general attacks on our forests cannot be stopped by artificial deterrence. If the pests come they will conquer or wear themselves out. We are helpless after they gain a strong foothold. State laws may do much but for the most part they can only save our wayside and lawn trees.

THE DECORATION OF ESTATES

THERE will be seen on page 280 an example of natural decoration found beside a little pass in Lyme. The growth of these cedars, very precisely vertical, and usually in finely symmetrical slender cones, is a notable characteristics of Connecticut landscapes. In their varying sizes on a rolling pasture, where they are always seen if at all, they afford amongst the great boulders and the short cropped grass a delightful study. A drive winding among such cedars is easily contrived so as to enhance the charm of the drive and that of the trees. Dwellings erected at the higher points of such pastures are just sufficiently screened by this scattering growth to be ideally attractive.

These cedars are never very large nor of great age but young trees, if allowed to sprout, will take the place of the old and there will be no conscious break in the beauty of such landscapes. We think that a judicious use of such pastures may open to the development of estates in Connecticut a very extensive and delightful improvement. This will be possible only if the pastures are left very nearly in their original state. There must be many thousands of sites of the highest merit within the limits of the state all beautifully covered with these naturally sprouting cedar decorations. We are very eager to see advantage taken of this waiting opportunity. The coast towns and great parts of the south-western portion of the state together with here and there considerable regions to the east and north afford these growths. There are parts of our country where an immense outlay would not be grudged to secure decorations. If we ask why the opportunity is not seized the answer appears to lie in the lack of knowledge of the average city man as to

THE ANNUAL REVIVAL—KENT

AN ORCHARD PATH—CHATHAM

TUMBLE DOWN DALE—KENT

when he is really in the country. In instances too frequent to count he secures a property on a main road, huddled between dwellings and with small chance of successful development. It is not, perhaps, to be wondered at that one who lived on a city street should suppose that one tree with a little plot of ground is country. Mark Twain was wise enough to go into a district in Connecticut, Redding, which had been neglected. There are still many portions of Connecticut where ten acres or a hundred even may be secured for the same charge made for a meagre lot in some of the fashionable villages of the state. We know of land changing hands at ten dollars an acre, every acre of which is from every aspect worth a hundred such acres in so-called improved locations.

Let no one in these times, when we have had a little leisure to examine the question what really constitutes a family seat, deceive himself by supposing that money will create such a seat. The money of a nabob will not build a hill or create a brook or successfully transplant a really noble tree. We have in mind at this moment a huge and rich structure erected on an absolutely bare plain in the country within a quarter of a mile of ideal locations. It is an outworn observation that many who know how to make money are not aware how they should spend it, nevertheless, when a wealthy man tries to be wise, as he undoubtedly does when he builds in the country, he needs help. He is willing too often to buy stones but not ideas. Of course, this is because he thinks his own thoughts are ideas. We know instances where locations were secured by correspondence, and with nothing in view except the distance from a certain railway station. Other inducements have been that some well-known family owned the estate next to that which the investor is purchasing. These considerations are petty in comparison with the broad purpose which ought to animate the development of a country place. The idea of high, well-drained grounds with good prospects, with a sheltering background, with splendid trees, with a stream or lake, with ample room to erect a dwelling far from the highway, all these are considerations which ought not to be omitted. Upon this foundation of combined ideas there is then an opportunity for a man who respects his generation and desires to found a family, or to continue a noble name, to provide himself a permanent dwelling which may pass down through a great many generations, who shall love it for its beauty, its healthful situation, its associations and its romance. On a prairie or a town lot romance is difficult, and will require a genius far beyond that of a person whose largest endowment is financial. We speak feelingly because all up and down Connecticut we see squandered a quantity of money ample for the purpose of securing results worth while. We have somewhere said and say again after mature deliberation, that a billion a year and perhaps now as much more, is annually expended on dwellings, and mostly wasted.

Landscape gardeners have, sometimes by their education and sometimes by their practice, been confined to the development of small areas. When a broad state is considered, as the bound within which choice is to be made, the opportunity is too rich to permit narrow views. It is a very narrow view to locate according to present fashion. An individual estate, if it is large, may be many miles removed from a fashionable quarter and be of no less value intrinsically or socially, because the present means of movement are so facile that what would have been isolation is no longer so. In fact, one cannot conceive of any large estate possible in Connecticut that could now be called isolated. Generations pass so rapidly, and a local vogue so much more rapidly, that the only sane consideration in the location of a country place should be its absolute beauty and dignity. The imagination revels in the wonders that might easily be wrought by the combination of abundant with judicious expenditure on an estate, we will say, of a hundred acres or more, well chosen among the hills. Nor could the most thorough socialist object to the possession by one estate of so much ground, since ground unsuitable for cultivation is best adapted for such an estate. Many a poor farmer owns such a site, and, remaining on his few good acres, would dispose of the balance of his farm and remain where he is, a valuable ally, as a source of many country products that would be wanted as the new estate developed.

MEADOW WATERS — PORTLAND

SHARON BRIDGE

DOUBLE WALLED LANE—WINDHAM

THE BLOOMING MEADOW—NEWFIELDS

But we would not confine our suggestions to the few or to the wealthy. Old farms may be availed of by persons of small means who are yet able to erect little cottages in delightful retreats which, so far as romance and family traditions are concerned, may become just as dear to the coming generation as a formal and extensive mansion. In fact, with a humble beginning the development of the family fortunes may go on exhibiting themselves in an addition to the original cottage and then another addition, until a thoroughly charming sequence of wings of a room or two each may provide, perhaps, a dwelling place for one or more branches of the family and may have a charm exceeding that of a lofty, pretentious structure.

There are records in our memory of some such glades or crests or nooks. We see within seventy miles of New York a fine level bench ample for several dwellings though each took some acres for its grounds. There is a background of large and scattered trees and clumps of evergreen, and a second hill rises behind. In the foreground begins the slope to a wonderful valley divided into fields marked out by elms and oaks. In the mid-distance is a little river and far beyond there is the opposite crest of the valley.

We see another prospect waiting for generations. It is on the route from Danbury north. There is a semi-circular sweep of lofty hills, a broad stream in the foreground, a gentle rise between it and the evergreens on the steeps. On this gentle rise are here and there attractive trees. The whole area may be a matter of fifty acres more or less, absolutely satisfactory to the eye and to the feeling, yet of no great commercial value.

We see again, perhaps a hundred and twenty feet from the highway, a large and picturesque rambling dwelling with three or four immense trees. The site slopes gently. It occupies only an acre or two. It is near but not on a trolley line and sufficiently near to a local market town. We have watched this old house for twenty years. It has been allowed to fall into decay until this spring we observe that the roof on one section has fallen. Here was a location for people of limited means, such that every passer-by would have exclaimed at its beauty had it received even ordinary care and slight restoration. The amazing fact is that of the million passers-by in that time, many of them seeking country places, not one has had the vision to select it. It is a humiliating statement. We see again on a narrow bench below a very lofty hill a cottage site a little removed from the main highway so as to be possessed virtually of a private drive. This site offered nearly all the advantages which we have been recounting and went begging at a price less than a good mechanic could earn in a year.

We remember a dwelling some hundreds of feet from the street. Its hewn overhang and its fine steep roof placed it about the year 1700. It was of ample size and in fair condition and its grounds, of perhaps two or three acres, were exquisitely decorated with many great trees. A purchaser was sought for it and for years sought in vain, and at a price within the reach of any able-bodied person, not to mention those who then and since have expended ten times as much as would have been required here, and have secured what would not market today for the cost of the site that went begging. This particular site was a mile or two to market and the railway and within ten or fifteen miles of large cities by fine roads.

It is, perhaps, not desirable to catalogue more of the pictures that remain in our minds but are not otherwise recorded, yet we venture the bold assertion that we could select a hundred ideal sites a week. Most of these, it would be possible to supply with water flowing by gravity to all parts of a dwelling from a privately owned and controlled spring. All of them would be sufficiently roomy for the erection of a dwelling many rods from traffic. All of them would be agreeably broken in contour and all of them amply shaded and decorated by old and majestic growths. As the years go on we are increasingly amazed at the awful poverty of imagination which the American exhibits when he chooses his home. Any one who selects a bad site advertises himself as blind. We know when we

THE CORNER OF A COMMON—SOUTH WOODSTOCK

AN OLD CONNECTICUT INN—WOODSTOCK

BEYOND THE POND—WINDSOR

THE LITTLE PASS—LYME

see what he has done that there is only a small portion of the world that has ever opened upon him. The glories of the universe are shut away from him. He doesn't see the principal things of which life consists. Neither in his architecture nor in his location has he manifested wisdom, taste, thought or love for what is essentially lovely. Why waste time upon him? Well, many such persons, either by their lack of opportunity or their lack of natural taste, are not really deserving of a mad house or a jail. They only seem to be so.

A crusade for better things; hard blows, telling the truth about this state of things; and loud wails raised against it; possibly a little scorn thrown upon it, may arouse somebody to ask himself that first of all vital question: is it really necessary to look about a little in order to know something?

ALONG THE SOUND

LONG ISLAND SOUND, on both sides, has been preëmpted by those who enjoy the advantage of two modes of communication. These shore estates have the benefit of the beautiful Connecticut drives, and their power launches or yachts give them command of another great range of observation. Such places as the Anson Phelps Stokes estate at Noroton, while not common, are examples of the finer sort. Mr. Stokes, by the way, was much of a builder, and created the great estate in the Berkshires, afterwards owned by Carnegie. Owing to an accident in which he lost a leg, he removed to the Sound where, since he could no longer ride, he could sail.

Some great hotels, as those out of New London, have observed the strategic advantage of the shore. Innumerable little bays or estuaries abound along the Sound. We are more fond of a bold coast than of the more usual gentle slopes of the Sound. Occasionally where the estuaries come into the hills, as at Westport and on the Thames, there is the advantage of sites on fine bluffs looking down upon the placid reaches of the narrow waters, which are more beautiful than the broader Sound, and are, of course, immediately in connection with the Sound.

Connecticut escapes, for the most part, the flamboyant shore resorts seen so often on the New York end of the Sound. As New York City men have often retained their original residences in Connecticut, and use them for all-the-year homes, especially for the first fifty miles from the state line, the state has the advantage of whatever inspiration the metropolis may supply in the way of architectural suggestion. Further, it has benefited by its nearness to New York in the spread of wealth expended upon country estates in this section.

Wherever the land and sea meet there is romance. The shores are here and there dotted with memorials of British descents from the time of the Revolution or the War of 1812. There is a monument at Groton of such a descent and attack. Smuggling, also, in the old days, though it has lost its flavor, except for the far less romantic work of the rum-runner, has left some traditions along the shore. One who is a novice in Connecticut may suppose himself to have seen the Sound roads by passing over the main line from New York to Rhode Island. As a matter of fact, in this journey the Sound is generally out of sight. There are so many streams to cross that the main road called the Boston Post Road goes from point to point of the old bridges or ferries at the head of the estuaries. In order, therefore, to see the Sound country with any degree of thoroughness one must follow to the various necks or peninsulas, either circling back by some other road or in the case of long and narrow spits of land, returning as he went. Rhode Island has lured away the Connecticut people who desire a very bold marine outlook, and at Watch Hill she possesses the last great rocks on our coast as one goes south and west. The people of Connecticut, however, are very fond of their own shore lines, and many ancient estates are found on these tortuous littorals. Lyme, New London, Stamford, Greenwich and many other shore towns were founded at the very beginning of American settlements and here and there we find a dwelling built in the seventeenth century. Wherever we do discover an original Con-

A COLONIAL STREET—MIDDLE HADDAM

THE BUTTONBALL BOUGH—NEW MILFORD

NUTTINGHAME IN SPRING

ALL CURVES—SOUTHBURY

necticut family in this district we find a conservative family and usually one of much capacity, which it has demonstrated by its ability to hold its own through ten generations. Such a family will have its ancient trees, its original boat landing and its old farm drives, all giving a flavor of independence, antiquity and beauty.

There are families of this sort who dwell in homes composed of huge oak timbers and containing looking glasses bought in Venice in the beginning of the eighteenth century, with native furniture of a still earlier period. Not a few of the ancestors of these families were seafaring men, who brought from the ends of the earth various useful or curious spoils. Thus, here and there, one finds teakwood from India and Chinese cabinets and Japan lacquer. Italy and Turkey have contributed to the plenishing. It gives one a sense of the romantic and the ancient day to live in the midst of such heirlooms. Thus the old trees over the old houses filled with the old furnishings and haunted by the old traditions supply an unmistakable atmosphere that cannot be duplicated in the newer parts of our country, or indeed when one leaves the salt-water line. The sturdy founders of these homes often built their own ships before they sailed them, and the great war here and there revived that industry for the time being. Along this coast the submarines and such novel craft possessed the minds of Connecticut inventors.

The possession of a power launch of good size opens to these shore residents excursions of the most interesting sort. Without going outside the limits of the Sound they have, on the two shores, many hundreds of miles of beauty to explore. Sometime we hope to devote more attention to Long Island and to give greater prominence to that road of the seventeenth century, the Sound. Any state with a sea line partakes something of the character of ancient English independence because it may, if it has the genius, master both sea and land. Besides, it isn't necessary actually to incur the risks of a sea voyage. Seated in one's den overlooking the waves, one may sail with Raleigh or Drake or the clipper skippers and weather, without water or blood, the storms and battles of the days when men were out not so much for prizes as for adventures. In fact, it is always a calamity to lose the adventurous spirit. Those ancients dared upon the sea. We think that at the present time history would become more piquant and society richer if we dared more greatly in enterprises that were not altogether commercial. There is always such a delight in undertaking new things, even when our efforts fail. At least we have the experience and the joy of trying. For instance, somebody might try to reform the legislative system of Connecticut; someone might carry through a law to make it a crime to build wooden chimneys; someone might start a line of steamships to a country not directly tied by such communication with America; someone might try to rejuvenate our railroads; and someone might study until he knew the old life well enough to write a novel that should not be full of anachronisms. This last is something that nobody has done yet, at least in America. There is plenty of courage required in a time of peace and plenty in undertaking to finish the country. Also, there are plenty of Connecticut men with genius to accomplish these things. They love their gardens too well and the wide world too little, perhaps.

After many of our great wars, a new spirit of adventure or discovery or invention or a new outburst of genius has been manifested. We await such an event in the more conservative sections of America. The most and the worst that has happened up to the present time is the declination of men to work, as if this were a new departure. There are several things still to be done, like the uniting of the Christian denominations and the simplification of the laws. These things are revolutionary to be sure but when we get beyond the period of revolutions the world is too tame.

AN ALL-THE-YEAR COTTAGE—RIDGEFIELD

THE COUNTRYSIDE—MIDDLETOWN

SKY BROOK—KENT   BLOSSOM RILL—NORFOLK

UNRECOGNIZED BEAUTIES

THE other day we called at a beautiful old place which invited us by a ribbon drive, buttonwood trees, and with an enormous tree of that sort at the gable of the house. As we turned toward the barnyard we noticed its huge stone wall curving at the corners and flanked by splendid elms. The barn, at the peak of the gable, was arranged with a dove cote, and over the great doors there were also, almost in the form of a transom, pigeon holes. It was altogether the most attractive farmyard, taken as a whole, that we have ever seen. As we stood admiring it, the camera in my hand and a case of plates in Teeta's, we became aware that the housewife was looking at us around the corner. We said, " What a beautiful farmyard! " She made no reply at first and we returned to the mention of the attractions before our eyes. At last she said: " It is no prettier than other people's." What a pitiful thing it is that people look beyond them, when here was a composition which might have been sought, and sought in vain, by city dwellers, who would be willing to spend a great deal of time and money, to secure effects as good and as natural. The housewife, in this case, even seemed suspicious that we were poking fun at her. All this would not be so saddening were it exceptional. It is, however, the rule that the owners of the most attractive farmsteads have never suspected that they were beautiful. We recall instances in almost every county in New England of country places that arrest the attention owing to the beautiful combination of fences, dwellings, trees, lanes or gardens, in all which cases the owners have never thought of their homesteads as forming harmonious unities. Very likely they fuss over a little front yard and might admit that some white blossoming bush or peony was pretty. But the effect, as a whole, they almost never admire. There are such homesteads, pictures of which have become known throughout the land for their beauty, though the very owners themselves have not yet learned how much pleasure their work has given, nor are they at all conscious of any merit in it.

The most successful work we have ever done was about homes that had never appealed to their owners. They have been the only surprised persons when, as is sometimes the case, they have seen pictures of their premises.

We imagine that artists from the beginning of time have drawn subjects that perhaps have achieved a world-wide reputation without any recognition, by the persons most intimately concerned, of the beauty, the allurement, the sentiment expressed in the outlines of their homesteads or their home brooks or orchards or highways.

What can be done to overcome this blindness to beauty? How important it is to overcome appears when we consider how enriched country people are when they do finally awake to the unfelt attractions about them. Aroused to a world of beauty in their immediate vicinity, they are taught the most important thing in education, namely, that they already dwell in heaven; that it isn't necessary to go to some high view point or to some celebrated scene. Those very notable points are as a rule avoided by artists. Pass through any great art gallery and it is very exceptional to find a trite and much advertised scene. It is the homely, the simple and the near that is really the attractive and satisfactory in art. This is the saddest and worst heathenism, to push God afar off.

It would be doing the greatest service to any country community should someone with an eye for beauty go through the neighborhood, and record a few of its attractions, and then call that neighborhood together and tell them that they were living in the midst of delights untasted. Such knowledge elevates human sentiment and brings joy and a sense of quickened appreciation. Chiefly, perhaps, future good will come out of awakening people to look and seek for loveliness everywhere. How many millions there are who wish they might go to Washington or to Paris or at least to Niagara or the mountains. Great artists, however, flee the cities to get into the very neighborhood of these discontented ones. The most awful heresy that can come into a life is to imagine that man can make anything

ELM SILHOUETTES — MANCHESTER

MILFORD IN THE HILLS

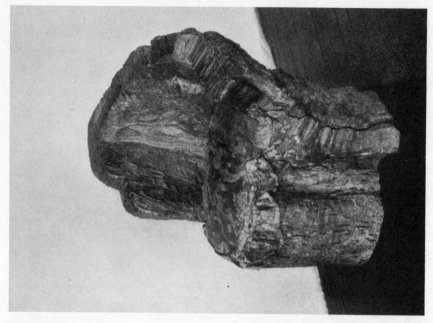

CHARTER OAK CHAIR

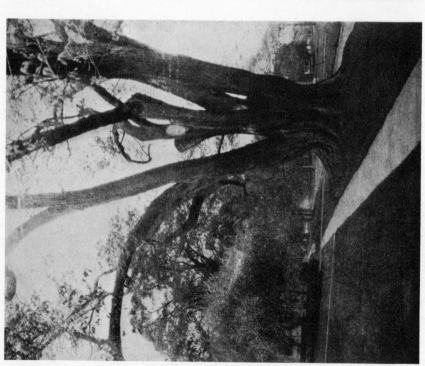

THE GREAT WETHERSFIELD ELM

as beautiful or as perfect as God has made. If we just knew this we should not be so feverishly seeking what men have done. In fact, the men who have done most are those who have gone to nature and not forsaken her. In short, when we find what men have done, it would appear that those who have done anything worth while have listened at the heart of nature. If there is anything in Paris or Rome to see, it was brought in from the country, or it was copied from a human face, or it was suggested by the leaf, or the flower, or the arch of the forest. Men are copying, in their carving, motives as old as history. Possibly some soul large enough and simple enough will sometime arise to incorporate into our architecture the flowers of the field, as they grow here.

There have been some attempts at model villages. We think that such a village might be created that would do far more good than the same expenditure on any other object. The models that we have seen were rather slight and especially lacked in the element of permanence. And amongst all the models that have come to our attention we have never yet seen a successful attempt to erect a country farmstead in its entirety and in a permanent form.

We see on every hand, from city to city, great school halls, on which very much skill has been exercised. But are there not many more who live in simple homes than who attend schools with such halls? Might not the states, who are making pets of their universities, supply in every county or at least in some one county, a farmer's residence built as it should be, and having contiguous to it its beautiful and necessary farm buildings?

What we need is not more homes but better homes. If, as not seldom occurs, the new home is worse than the old, why this universal fever for home building? It would appear as if a bare thought without its proper outlines had seized the American mind. We build first and think afterwards. At least this might be done and done at once, so that the site and the dwelling may be harmonious.

SUPPER–TIME

By Mildred Hobbs

(For the picture of Sheep on page 88)

Twilight in the valley,
Streaked with purple haze!
Sunset on the hillside,
And the pasture all ablaze!
Drowsy sheep stand waiting
For the master's call,
And run to him with bleating cries
When the long bars fall.

Tinkle of the cowbell,
Lowing of the cows!
Frisking of the sheep dog
If they tarry long to browse,
Straying and delaying
On the homeward way,
For here a tuft of tender grass,
There a tempting spray!

Supper-time and greetings —
Clucking, clacking hens,
Sleepy little lambkins,
And the old farm denizens
Gather at the manger
At the close of day.
And once, among such friends as these,
The baby Jesus lay.

SUMMER WEALTH—BROAD BROOK

THE CHARTER OAK

INDEX